001 — TATJANA HAUPT / TATI THINGS — DEU — THE POWER OF MY HANDS

THE POWER OF MY HANDS is a celebratory homage to the designers German grandmother, who was a typical subordinate housewife, and her punk mother, who was a pioneer in the male dominated world of IT. Together they taught her the importance of being oneself and standing up for women's rights. Through her knitwear she is looking into traditional craftsmanship and its relation to politics. Throughout the process she asks the question: How can feminism be expressed through craft today? Photographed by Anna W. ↦ see also p. 3

MESSAGE

A T-shirt is a billboard. Most of the time, it has some nonsense written on it. Relax California Camp David Beach Love. Or Keep Calm and some bullshit. And protests shirts. Lots of protests. Simple, bold, in-your-face. Like a Poster.

PROTEST
CLAIM
THOUGHT
POLITICS
ETHICS

TATI THINGS
ENGELHARDT
DERNAI
BELA
POUSSIN
VVVVV
DORN
HORVÁTH
GRÜTZNER
MÄDER
CHIN
STUDIO NIKOLAI DOBREFF
LAVENDER
SCHÜLLER
STUDIO MICHAEL SATTER
FETANIS

002—FLORIAN ENGELHARDT—DEU—MAKE MASCULINITY OBSOLETE ↓
An increasing number of people—mostly men—have felt threatened by critical voices questioning the conventional concept of the term. "Make masculinity great again" is often used as their slogan—an unmistakable homage to the former US president Donald Trump, a man who arguably embodies the conventions more than anyone else. This work is a comment on this phenomenon. The message is not just to question the concept of masculinity but rather to argue that we should get rid of it completely. This work was created as part of Klasse Roberts at ABK Stuttgart.

003—LENA ZOE DERNAI—DEU—BETWEEN PROTEST AND POETRY ↑
BETWEEN PROTEST AND POETRY is a flexible protest-kit comprised of jackets with a hanging system and removable cardboard letters—making it easy to create different messages as forms of demonstration or daily poetry.

004—NADINE BELA—DEU—PUBLIC PROPERTY

This project delves into the themes of objectification and sexual harassment in public spaces using tights inscribed with PUBLIC PROPERTY. The provocative inscription aims to unsettle, mirroring the discomfort of being objectified, as though privacy is lost and one's body is no longer one's own. It symbolises the violation of boundaries and the enduring impact of objectification, persisting even beyond the tights.

005——ISMAHANE POUSSIN——WAGE AGAINST THE MACHINE——FRA

WAGE AGAINST THE MACHINE is a hybrid project between typographic and artistic research practice, enhanced by Ismahane Poussin. When she began her project, her goal was to repurpose the tools of fashion, specifically knitting, to create a space for typographic and protest expression, exploring the intersection of patterns and letters with messages against fast fashion. Knitted on hacked knitting machine, Brother KH910 with Ayab. ↦ see also p. 7, 61

006—STÉPHANIE VILAYPHIOU / VVVVV—BEL—MY MOTHER WAS A COMPUTER ↓

This project is a series of portraits of women who had a major role in the history of computing. "Computers" used to design women whose job was to calculate, to compute. When the first computers were invented, women were put onto the machines to manipulate them. Once men grasped the potential of computing, they took over women's place. Knitted on hacked knitting machine, Brother KH940 with Ayab, the font in use is *Combine* by Julie Pa.

007—MAIKE C. DORN—
DEU—RISE UP!

In a patriarchal system there is no justice for those affected by patriarchal violence. RISE UP!—knotted wall hanging, 95 cm × 35 cm.

008—ANNA HORVÁTH—HUN—MAKING MY FIRST ZINE TOOK A LOT OF TIME

After years of design education, the artist finally made her first zine. To do this, she chose a time-consuming, monotonous technique: knitting. The pages of the zine illustrate the stages of the process and convey a sense of the time spent knitting.

009—TIM GRÜTZNER—DEU—MANIFEST VOM PFAU. AMAZING! AMAZING?

The focus of the intervention lies on the interaction with customers of Primark. The artist offers to buy the customers purchases as they leave the store. In return they will be rewarded with a refund, which equals the buying price plus 5€ on top. If the costumers agree to this deal, they will have to hand over all of their purchases including the receipt. At the end of the day all of their purchases will be returned to the store.

01.0— MÄDER DEU IN

MAX —MADE IN BANGLADESH

MADE IN BANGLADESH emerges as a pivotal installment within the ongoing series titled *Made in*, a conceptual exploration that boldly brings the ostensibly concealed fine print into prominence on a grand scale. MADE IN BANGLADESH challenges the viewer to confront the ubiquitous but often overlooked labeling found on consumer goods and foregrounds the production facility.

011—SHIN-HEE CHIN—USA—MOTHER TONGUE AND FOREIGN LANGUAGE

In a mother tongue, one finds identity. It is natural, familiar, and easy. A foreign tongue feels unnatural, strange, and clumsy. Everything about a foreign tongue, especially when one deals with East versus West, is alien—alphabet, grammar, culture, and flavor. When one identifies a mother tongue, any other language becomes the "other."

012—STUDIO DOBREFF—DEU—NIKOLAI—FCK NZS

Football scarves are made for supporters and statements. This scarf supports democracy and stands against racism and Nazis. The message: "SCHEISS NAZIS" is German for "FUCK NAZIS."

013—MAXIME A. METZELER / BELLAVENDER—CHE—BOOK OF LIFE

Maxime-Alexandre Metzeler is a 22-year-old artist and designer from Zurich, Switzerland. In this project he illustrates his love for metaphors and proverbs, that often serve as a starting point in his design process. This handmade 1/1 outfit is built around a jacket that features 10 of the artists favorite proverbs: While the outside is inspired by book cover designs, the lining of the jacket features a sheet of paper-like material, printed with the proverbs that inspired the artist.

Ne juge jamais un livre par sa couverture,
suppose qu il y reste des choses à découvrir.
Des belles paroles, rarement vrai.
Des vrais mots souvent laids

Vouloir oublier c'est y penser sans cesse
Les choses changent quand le temps presse.
Guérison mérite patience, croissance.
Hélas, seuls les choix permettent
La vie, un jeu auquel tous sont acteurs
Derrière son masque,
personne ne suit les mêmes valeurs.
La vie serte ne sera pas que bonheur
Partager vos douleurs
afin de protéger votre cœur.

Les richesses d'autrui, délaissent ton regard
Concentre-toi sur la tienne,
écris ton histoire.
La vérité est plurielle,
les perspectives jamais universelles
Contente-toi d'avoir moins tort,
c'est ça l'essentiel.

Il ne s'agit pas d'avoir le jeu le plus fort
simplement de jouer ces cartes
avec un coup fort

L'histoire s'écrit en tournant les pages

014—JELENA SCHÜLLER—DEU—FAST FASHION FACTS ↓

Information and facts related to fast fashion, ironically captured on a very common fast fashion item: the T-shirt. Using a laser cutter, the message is revealed by burning letters and shapes into the fabric, encouraging people to reflect on consumer habits and highlighting the importance of sustainability.

015—MICHAEL SATTER / STUDIO MICHAEL SATTER—DEU— LIVE FROM EARTH × MICHAEL SATTER ↖

The collection draws inspiration from slogans sprayed on walls during the 1968 Paris student revolts, critiquing societal structures. A word mark featuring the Arabic Live From Earth logo and the slogan "Le trois mai 1968 Université Paris-Sorbonne" was designed. Playfully distorted using a photocopier, it resulted in various versions.

016—IOANNIS FETANIS—GRC—COOO ↗

As a passionate designer living in Greece, he spends more than 250 sunny days in his Athens office. However, he enjoys approximately 25 sunny days out of the office on a Greek island. The CURRENTLY OUT OF OFFICE hat is for every creative mind who wants to convert sunshine into a day off! Put on that damn hat whenever it feels right!

A–O

ALL-OVER

The all-over print is like camouflage where everything disappears. Even a dripping ketchup stain goes unnoticed. You disappear into the all over, like a soldier in his camouflage blending seamlessly into the landscape. It's only when you focus on a small section that you realize there's something more—that something is actually written there.

PRINT
FULL
PATTERN
TAPESTRY

FERENCZ
VAN BEIRENDONCK
STUDIO MELLI
FECHNER
CK MAURER
FANG
KRIKLII
ESTUDI TONI BAUZÀ
KOERS
BAKONYI
CBR
MUSA DEL ASFALTO
JANSEN
DONATH
M0D44
HOFFMANN
LOTTER
MOST
SCHRÖDER
CAL CHARACTERS
ODY&FORMA
KLUMP
TUDIO TEMP
STUDIO LUCAS HESSE
ZINSKI
NOSO
EGUCHI
T PRINT
WORDSHAPE
WEEKEND ROMANCE

017——BORBALA FERENCZ
——HUN——THE RETURN OF THE SHREDS

This collection is inspired from the waste that the fashion industry creates. Shreds from second-hand clothes are upcycled and given a new preciosity. The silhouette of the outfits are inspired from 17th century royal garments, in contrast with today's fast fashion items.

018—OMID NEMALHABIB / STUDIO MELLI—NLD—1401

1401 is a poster-calendar-blanket design that tells a new visual story with every date and event of the year. It also captures and combines typography with art, science, philosophy, and astrology, inspired by a range of fascinating Persian books and old manuscripts.

019—DENNIS FECHNER—BEL / DEU—CYANOTYPE SCARVES

A series of ten cyanotype scarves were designed, produced and tailored by hand with fully analog methods. On the fabric itself, you can see the shadows of written letters, addressed to a person called Esther. Some letters are readable, other parts are more abstract and reduced to a purely typographical interpretation. Each of the ten scarves has its own part of Esther's story. Cyanotype is a chemical process and early form of photography in which UV light transferred negatives to the textiles.

The fashion industry is a master at weaving narratives that sell not just garments but ideals—promising us a slice of originality, authenticity, and even concepts like peace, love, and sustainability. Slogans on clothing collections serve as powerful marketing tools, luring consumers with the allure of social responsibility and moral virtue. Yet, beneath the surface, questions linger about the tangible impact of these messages and the authenticity of mass-produced fashion.

021—DUOLIN FANG—USA—ANIMAL FARM

Just as Tetsuya Ishida portrayed Japan's lost decade, contemporary Chinese youth have opted for passive resistance, adopting a laid-back approach in the face of existential anxiety. They are reluctant to immerse themselves in work, eschew romantic pursuits, encounter challenges in acquiring homes, and harbor little hope for starting families. Modern anxiety permeates every aspect of life, intensifying as the challenges of existence become increasingly daunting.

022—SOFIA KRIKLII—KAZ—WITHOUT WORDS

The designer's work is a symbol of the devaluation of language and words in the modern world. Inspired by Picasso's painting *Guernica* and posters by Peter Bankov, their graphics convey the experience of war, where the language of visual expression becomes more powerful than words. These works do not contain phrases or inscriptions. The graphics are printed on plastic clothes, creating the effect of a transparent layer. This symbolizes the imprint of chaos and suffering on our daily lives.

023 — ESTUDI BAUZÀ — ESP
TONI — OFICI

OFICI (meaning "job" in the Catalan language) is the title of the latest album by the Mallorcan group CABOT. For the cover artwork, the team has worked with the concept of traces of creativity on work clothes: traces of paint, calligraphic song titles, dripping, etc., to transform everyday work into art.

024—ILYA KOERS—BEL—THE HUNT

For this project, Ilya Koers created live visuals in TouchDesigner, combining typography and hunting imagery. The project was inspired by a fascination with the purity and focus inherent in hunting scenes. The typography that emerged from this combination of images and words was screen-printed onto T-shirts.

025—KITTI BAKONYI—HUN—RETHINK

The hand-knitted typographic vest is titled RETHINK, with the letters "RE" on the back depicted as a barcode, alluding to today's mass-produced garments and their standardized appearance. On the front of the vest, the word "THINK" appears in a difficult-to-read, jumbled pattern, reflecting customs of the past. The project aims to raise awareness of the importance of rethinking garment production and the path toward a more sustainable future.

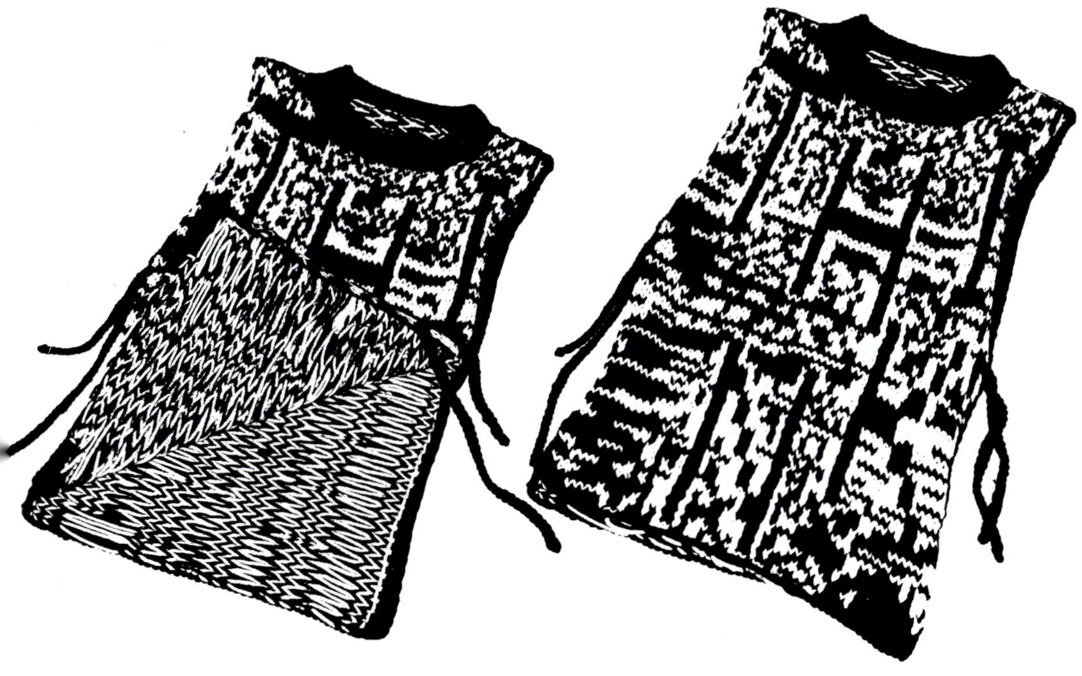

026——CHAE BYUNGROK / CBR——KOR——LAYERS-TYPEWORK

LAYERS makes garments and textiles that reflect a lifestyle of culture and style. Through an interpretation of Eastern typography and visual language, LAYERS crafts unique, civilized designs for inspired people.

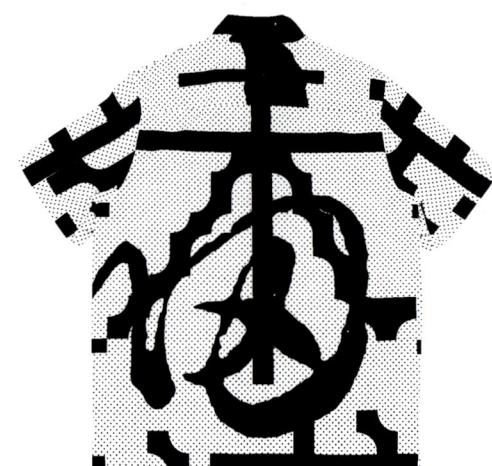

027—MUK MONSALVE, LUCHEE SOTO / MUSA DEL ASFALTO—ARG—COLECCIÓN LETRA CAPITAL & MADRE PATRIA

Musa del Asfalto is a brand of typographic scarves. This project derives from a sister project called *Letra Capital: Our Typewalk Tours in Buenos Aires*. The overall designs are inspired by the discoveries while researching and conducting tours. The lush landscape and letters of Buenos Aires became the designer's muse. The kerchief is not only a fashion accessory, but also a vessel for deeper meaning. The designers view their relationship to the city as a correspondence—and these scarves are a love letter to it.

028—MARIE JANSEN, PAULA DONATH—DEU—AFFIRMATIONS

We often feel frustrated with ourselves, yet we rarely speak positively to ourselves or find inner peace. AFFIRMATIONS are designed to change that. This project explores the use of tree affirmations in an experimental manner. The principle of repetition was applied within an animation and its boundaries were examined. Individual still frames from the animations were then further processed. The outcome includes three knitted blankets measuring 185 × 150 cm.

029—ANTON M0D44—DESIGNS

ABO/ M0D44

UKR FOR

Graphics for the Kyiv workwear brand M0D44. Industrial aesthetics, Post-Soviet visual noise, East European mess, Western trends—all this mixes up, mutates, and boils.

030—FRANÇOISE HOFFMANN—FRA—MODE D'EMPLOI

Françoise Hoffmann creates original hybrid "nuno" textiles, combining felt—handmade with a mix of carded wool fibers—and silk. After spending several years learning traditional felt, she started inventing her own new techniques. By playing with textures, materials, color, and prints, as well as her own photographic work, she explores a wide and varied artistic vocabulary. Photographed by Aldo Paredes.

031—HOFFMANN FRA

FRANÇOISE —TLEMCEN

Françoise Hoffmann creates original hybrid "nuno" textiles, combining felt—handmade with a mix of carded wool fibers—and silk. After spending several years learning traditional felt, she started inventing her own new techniques. By playing with textures, materials, color, and prints, as well as her own photographic work, she explores a wide and varied artistic vocabulary. Photographed by David Desaleux.

032—ANNIKA LOTTER—DEU—JUNGES BLUT

In response to the climate strikes, this project delves into the aspirations of the younger generation. Central to this exploration is the tension between self-discovery and the forging of a new collective identity. By uncovering the influence of generational paradigms, the project reveals how youth movements intertwine politics with fashion history. The culmination of this work includes three prints and eight outfits, each intricately designed to symbolize distinct themes through fabric patterns and cuts that mirror data visualizations.

033—KUBA SOWIŃSKI / MOST—POL—KIMONO

The jacquard fabric for this kimono was woven with cotton yarns, so despite being thick, it is very cozy. The jacket was made from different variations of the textile. The project is the result of the cooperation between the decorative textile studio MOST with Kuba Sowiński, an acclaimed Polish designer and assistant professor at the Faculty of Graphics at the Academy of Fine Arts in Kraków. "Woven fragments of official forms are our mischievous answer to the oppression of everyday existence," he states.

035 — MARY Y. YANG / RADICAL CHARACTERS, CHEN LUO / BODY&FORMA — USA — EMBODIED MAKING AS COLLECTIVE PUBLISHING: THE BODY AND HANZI

These wearable posters are artifacts from a workshop that explored the relationship between the body and Hanzi (Chinese characters). Participants practiced writing Hanzi at a large scale using the body as a canvas through a series of collaborative hands-on exercises. What are ways we can examine the boundaries between bodies and print, typography, and space, and the individual to the collective? What does collective publishing look like through collaborative labor in a shared space and time?

036—STELLA KLUMP—DEU— MATTER & MEANING—A RESEARCH ON TEXT AND TEXTILE TOWARDS ALTERNATIVE FASHION PERSPECTIVES.

The publication MATTER & MEANING explores the relationships between the textual and the textile. It consists of an accumulation of 50 texts from art and design research and conceptual design approaches that address the urgency of a new fashion system. The texts of the book form the pattern for four self-made garments—a top, sleeves, trousers, and a skirt. The book is thus brought into the space performatively and ultimately incorporated back into the book.

037—STUDIO TEMP— ITA—VELO TEMP ↓
VELO TEMP is a Studio Temp side project. VELO TEMP's goal is to use cycling as a field of visual exploration.

038—LUCAS HESSE / STUDIO LUCAS HESSE— DEU—ROBERT JOHNSON ↑
New York ain't Berlin, Paris ain't Berlin, Frankfurt ain't Berlin—and neither is Offenbach. Yet they take pride in running a club for 23 years now that most of you wouldn't expect to be situated in Frankfurt's not so popular neighbor city.

039— PHILIP RUDZINSKI—DEU — HUMANISTAN

Collectively unsynchronized. The fine line between camaraderie and rivalry in competition. HUMANISTAN unites languages, scripts, and traditions through seams into a collage of unity and diversity.

040—RAYMUNDO T. REYNOSO—USA—TOO OBSCURE ↓

TOO OBSCURE is a line of streetwear that began as a commentary on appropriation in contemporary design. The line explores the current ease in the "clipartification" of any image found online, the seemingly infinite availability of freeware fonts, and the commodification of real and imagined signifiers from Southern California Chicanx / Latinx / Cholx culture.

041—YUKI KAMEGUCHI—JPN—YOKONIKAWA MX ↑

A long sleeve T-shirt for the Tokyo retail shop SAILOSAIBIN'S flagship YOKONIKAWA line, featuring hand lettering in the style of motocross jerseys.

042—TEST PRINT—CHE—TEST PRINTS ↓
TEST PRINT consists of five self-taught screen-printing friends, who carry out mandates for the art and design worlds as well as self-initiated projects. The mix between commissions and made-up visuals blurs the boundaries between these fields, and changing the status of the so-called test prints, which are the tests on prototype fabrics before the final prints, bringing them to the forefront and happily adding extra layers to them in order to achieve charged compositions bordering on abstraction.

043—IAN LYNAM / WORDSHAPE, SAMUEL RHODES / WEEKEND ROMANCE—JPN—TWO WAY TIE FOR LAST ↑
Finally, a shirt that you can read! Two Way Tie for Last is a zine in long sleeve tee shirt form. The debut issue—spanning TWO shirts—features a killer essay about Japanese convenience stores, lighting, the Olympics, and design, and a mini-essay about "innovation." The shirt includes a recommended listening playlist and heaps of new and old graphics by Ian and Sam, printed in fluorescent orange and reflex blue on heavy white Gildan long-sleeve shirts!

KNITTING

Back in the day, at university—even in some school classes—everyone was knitting. Knitting and crocheting were all the rage. Women even wore crocheted bikinis at the beach! Norwegian sweaters were the epitome of cool. Then came polyester, fleece, Gore-Tex, and computers. Now, working with analog materials is doubly chic!

**YARN
STITCH
GRANDMA
PATTERN
BLOCKING**

TYPEKNITTING
BEYELER
PFEUFFER
PORTNOÏ
MOST
SLEIMAN
WALSER
GRAMBOLE
HARTLEY
DEFEZ
OTOG STUDIO
LE GAL
MARC ARMAND WORKS
FEELINGS
WILL
VAN DE SEYP
NOBLE STORE
DOCTOR
FISCHER
KANNO
PARTERRE

044—RÜDIGER SCHLÖMER / TYPEKNITTING—CHE—TYPEKNITTING

Rüdiger Schlömer is a graphic designer, educator, and book author based in Zürich. With TYPEKNITTING, he explores the typographic potential of hand knitting techniques. As a dialog between digital typography / type design and the analog craft of knitting, this results in knitting patterns, posters, and typefaces. His book *Pixel, Patch und Pattern. Typeknitting* received a Certificate of Typographic Excellence from the TDC New York. He gives workshops in schools, museums, and at knitting festivals. Photography by Linda Suter. ↦ see also p. 48

045—FLORIAN BEYELER—CHE—BT FLIMMER SCARF

Keep yourself, your friends, your family, and your pets (?) warm with this eye-catching tricolor scarf. Displaying the potential of detailed and varied glyphs, the typeface *BT Flimmer* adorns this scarf with its unique letters. On one side, the letters are upscaled and shown only in fragments. On the other side, the full name of the typeface is written out. The tricolor scarf is knitted with green, white, and black acrylic yarn.

046—JULIUS PFEUFFER—DEU—KNITTED GLYPHS
In the attempt to leave no knitted glyph undiscovered, this fusion of programming and traditional craftsmanship emerged. Weaving a million character combinations into this distinctive tapestry.

047—NICOLAS PORTNOÏ—FRA—DO NOT TOUCH

This work is part of a series that draws parallels between the screen and knitting. Through a set of typographic experiments, the project questions the effect produced by using one or the other. Each piece is an occasion for the evocation or transposition of images from one medium to the other. This piece explors relief knitting, a technique used in sock making is employed to form 3D pixels, thus taking advantage of some of the possibilities offered by the knitted fabric.

048—KUBA SOWIŃSKI / MOST—POL—ROMEO AND JULIET

ROMEO AND JULIET, a jacquard cotton shawl, made for the decorative textile company MOST by Kuba Sowiński, an acclaimed Polish designer. ROMEO AND JULIET, the immortal story, is written in *Matrix* font and transformed into woven jacquard fabric. Is love beyond the grave? We don't know, but a sense of humor definitely is.

049——NADINE SLEIMAN
——DEU——DON'T GET
TOO COMFORTABLE

Step out of your comfort zone—even or especially when it feels difficult.

49

Type Fashion — Slanted #44

050—MARIE WALSER, LOUISA GRAMBOLE—DEU—KLEIDOGRAFIE—TYPOGRAPHIC EXPLORATION OF A LONG-SLEEVED SHIRT

Collaborating artists Marie Walser and Louisa Grambole combine their specialties by experimenting with the placement and design of typography on garments. Analog and experimental, they explore various methods of displaying letters, words, sentences, or even entire texts on different parts of a long-sleeved white shirt. Beyond traditional paper mediums, clothing opens up endless possibilities for playing with different materials, textures, and the dynamic relationship between text and body. Photographed by Lena-Marie Gribl, the models are Lars Beck, Emilio Sultan Dinta, Emily Folcher, and Anna Huschka.

hierbei nebensächlich
ist hierbei nebensächlich
Textes ist hierbei

051—PADDY HARTLEY—GBR—LUMLEY, SPRECKLEY DIPTYCH

LUMLEY: Vintage military uniform, appliqué, digital embroidery, digital print, pyrography. Interpreting stories of WW1 facial injuries, Paddy Hartley employs digital embroidery, appliqué, and pyrography to convey historical research on the remarkable birth of facial reconstructive surgery and the lives of the men who endured and lived with the consequences of the surgery. Collection of the Museum of Arts and Design, New York, USA.

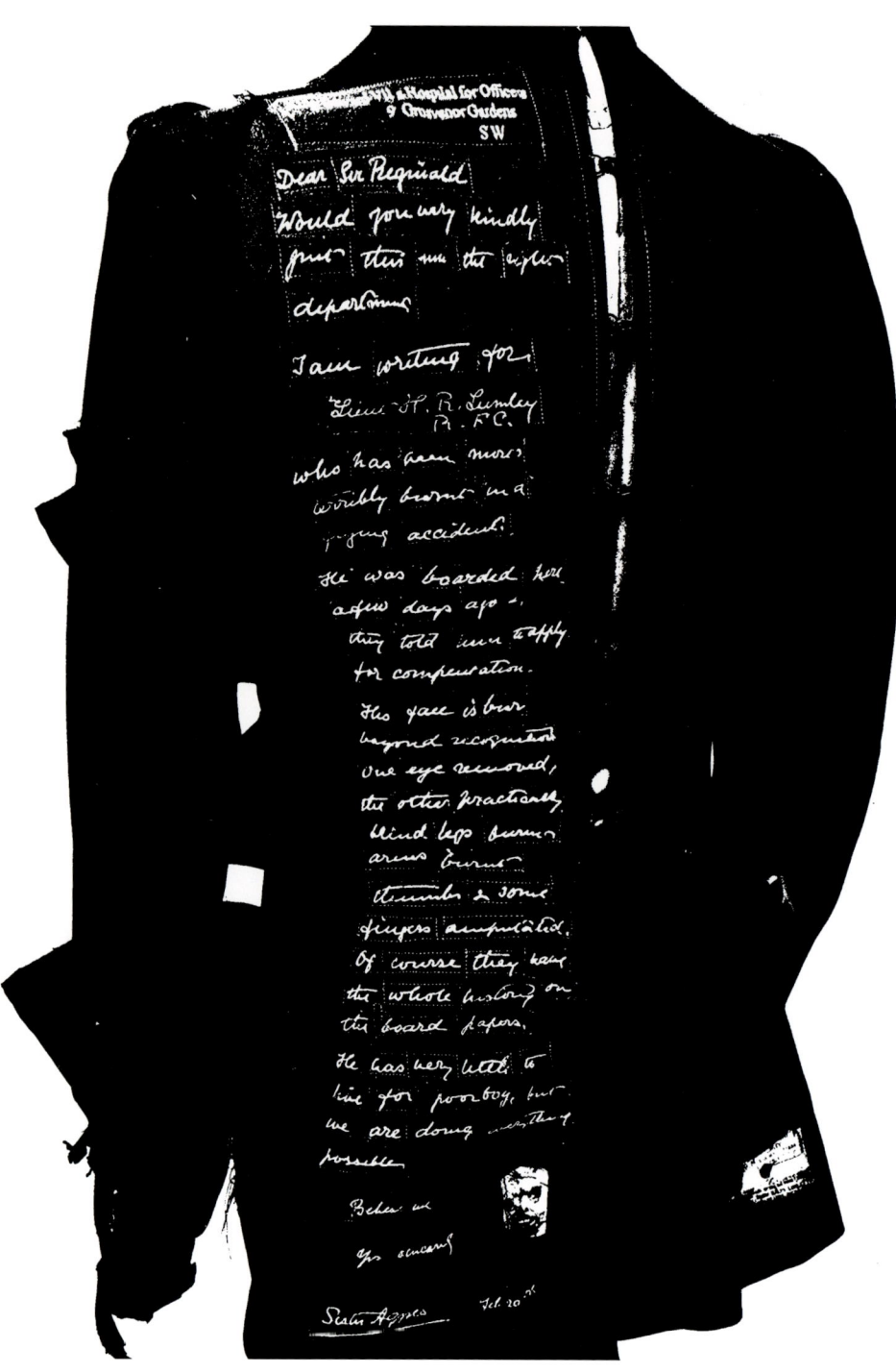

052—AURÉLIE DEFEZ—BEL —GENTRIFICATION SCARVES

This collection of scarves is inspired by a meme that states: "If you see this [object] in your neighborhood, your rent is about to increase." This series of scarves aims to humorously expose the reality that the work of designers in Western societies benefits from a strong emphasis on authenticity. Design pieces are typically accessible mainly to those with sufficient financial and / or cultural capital to acquire them, thus creating an element of exclusivity.

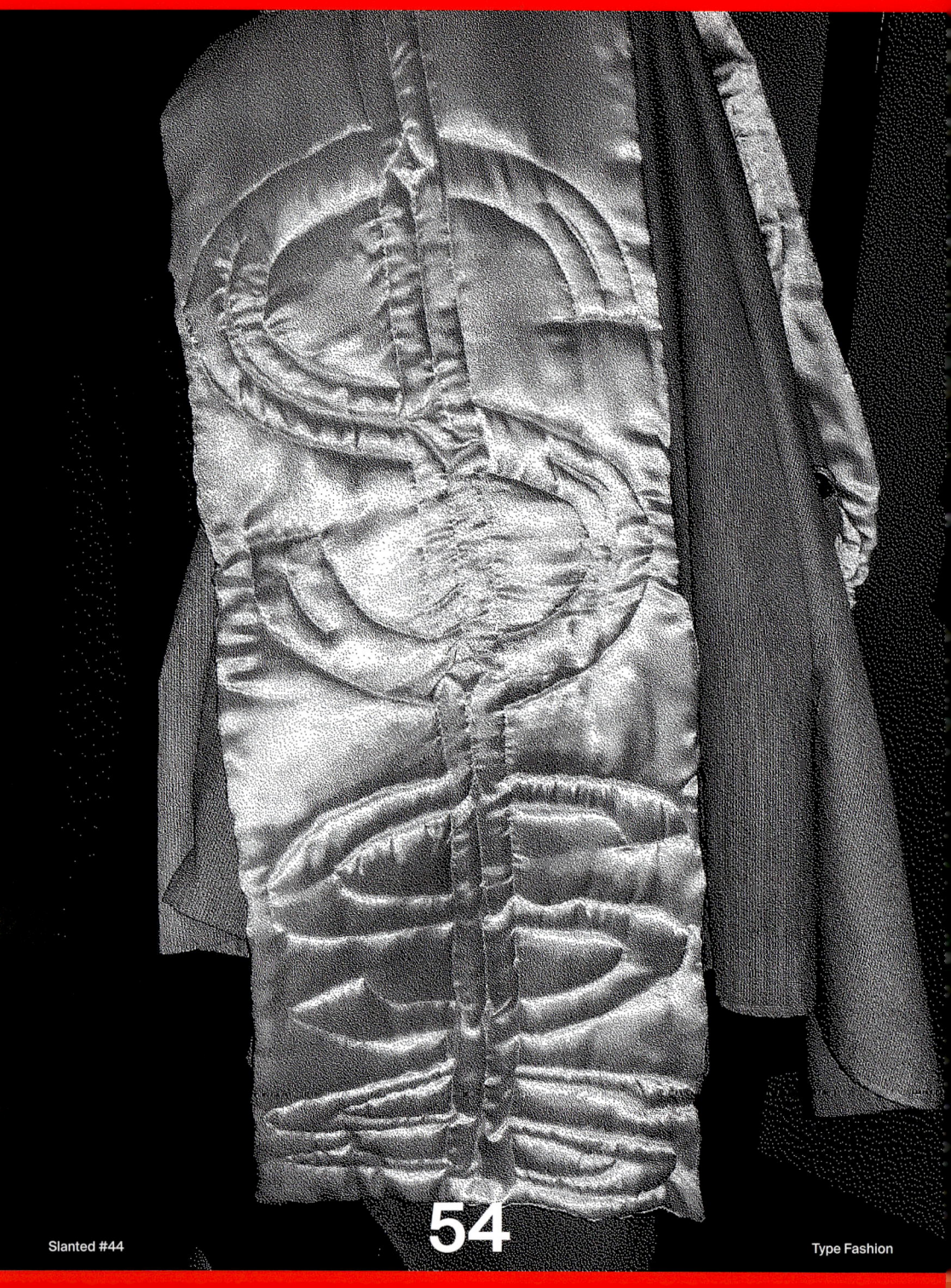

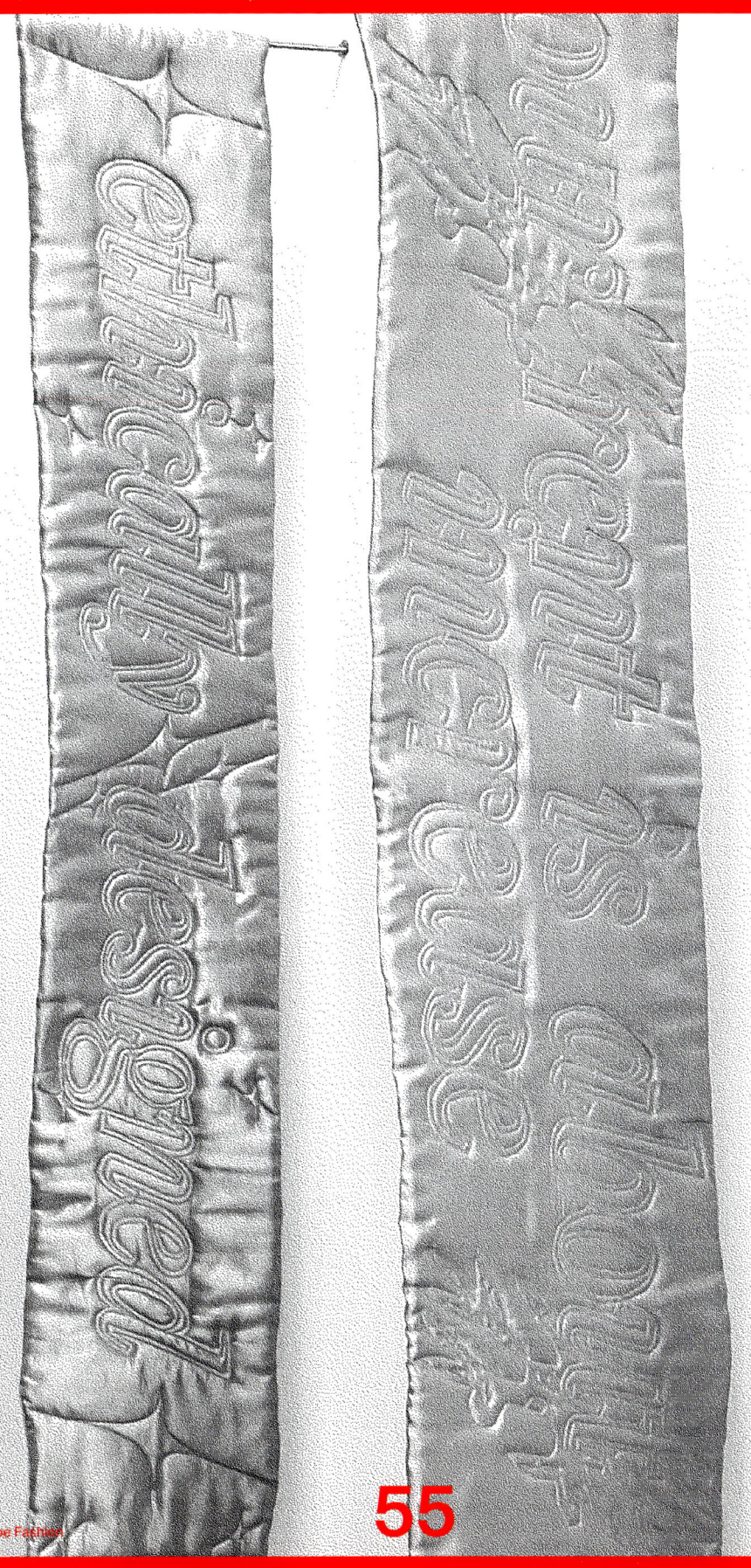

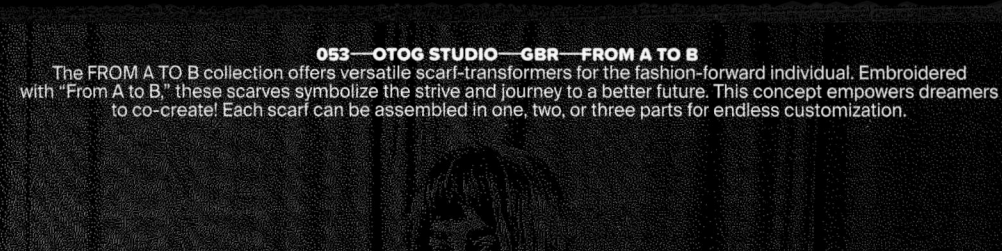

053—OTOG STUDIO—GBR—FROM A TO B

The FROM A TO B collection offers versatile scarf-transformers for the fashion-forward individual. Embroidered with "From A to B," these scarves symbolize the strive and journey to a better future. This concept empowers dreamers to co-create! Each scarf can be assembled in one, two, or three parts for endless customization.

054—LAURA LE GAL, MARC ARMAND / MARC ARMAND WORKS / FEELINGS—FRA—DRP POSTER FESTIVAL

DRP is a festival that celebrates urban culture and takes place in Paris. For this occasion, Marc Armand was commissioned to create the poster for the event. He chose to pay tribute to urban fashion, drawing inspiration from iconic fabrics and materials such as jacquard, puffer jackets, and all-over monograms. He created various DRP logos. Laura Le Gal then developed these logos into motifs and patterns on different materials, creating a collage reminiscent of a clothing market. The depicted work is not the final poster but rather showcases fabric experiments. Creative direction by Marc Armand Works / Feelings, with CGI art direction by Laura Le Gal.

055—BLANCA WILL—DEU—INSIDE OUT

This garment encourages you to turn your insides out, essentially sharing feelings and thoughts that we usually keep to ourselves. The inside out theme extends throughout the garment which is done in two ways: The garment itself is turned inside out showing the inner seams—so, the imperfect side with knots and loose threads points outwards. Additionally, the hand-embroidered word "inside" is also turned vice versa. It whoops: Show your beautiful mess! Words Clothes Expression, Communication Design project at Klasse Roberts, ABK Stuttgart; modeled by Svenja Will.

056—VERA VAN DE SEYP—NED / USA—MORF FORM

MORF FORM is a physical animation piece. It shows the word "MORF" transforming to "FORM" in three different phases. It was knitted on a hacked Brother knitting machine and the knitting pattern was generated from a knitting. The work was on display at ARTECHOUSE Miami during Art Basel Miami, 2023.

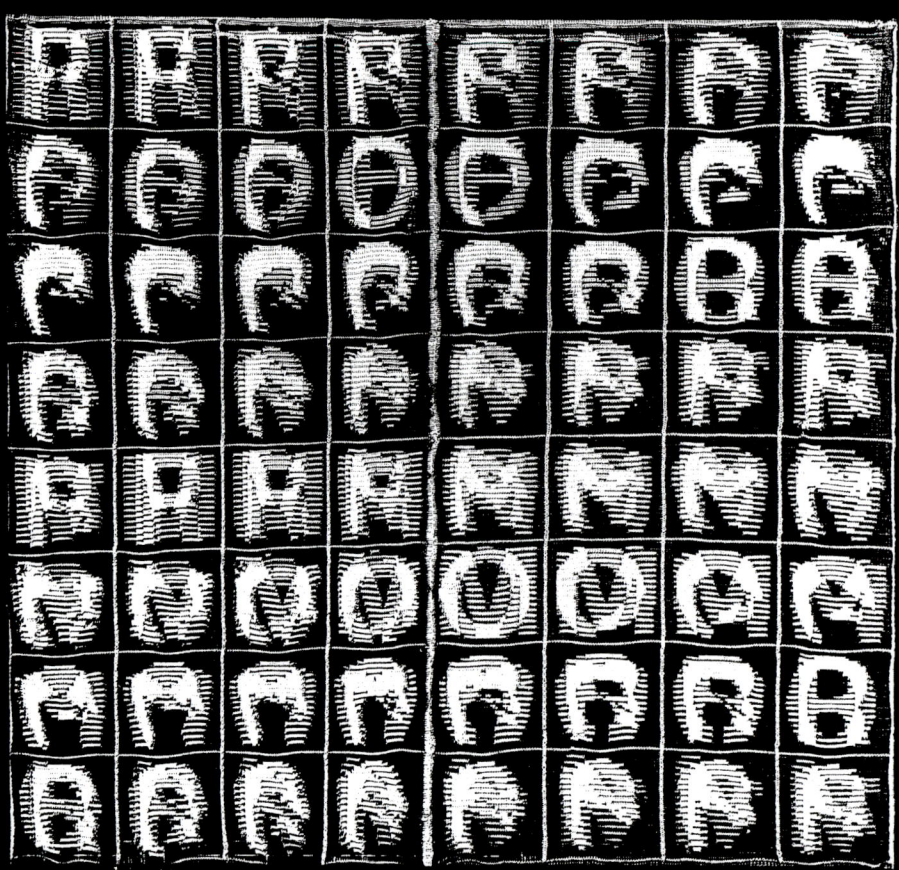

005 ↦ see p. 6

057—AMORE STORE—DEU—FC AMORE / TUTTO BENE, TAKE MY LOVE, AMORE PER TUTTI

Every season, Amore Store Berlin presents a special fan scarf collection, for which various renowned artists and designers contribute their creative designs. FC Amore Schal TUTTO BENE and TAKE MY LOVE by Kerstin Finger, FC Amore Schal AMORE PER TUTTI BY Jens Ludewig (Studio Bens) and Sarah Gottschalk (This is Jane Wayne).

058—MILAN DOCTOR, JONAS FISCHER—DEU—HEATSTROKE LIKELY
Milan and Jonas collaborated on the design of a custom scarf for their friends as a creative exercise. But caution is advised. The scarf is so hot and stylish, a heatstroke might be likely ;)

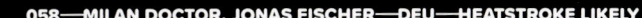

059— KONNO NDL—

LISA — BABA

BABA is a fashion collection and short film about Turkish immigrant Ceylan Utlu, by designer Lisa Konno and director Sarah Blok. Questions about the role of migration in his life, his relationship with his daughters, loneliness, and adaptation form the base of the story. The garments he wears in the film are inspired by his life story. The rug is used as a symbol of Orientalism, covered with wool prints illustrating his personal identity on top of what is perceived as Turkish.

060—KEVIN NOWAK / PARTERRE—AUT—KYTES FC SCARF

Design for German indie band KYTES. Part of their merchandise collection from the TO FEEL SOMETHING AT ALL Tour 2024. The artwork is based on a typographic approach and plays with the attributes of classic football merchandise.

ART

At art school, everything is allowed. On the runways too. It's called Haute Couture, as opposed to prêt-à-porter. In everyday life, all courage fades away. Anything that's a bit out of the ordinary is then simply called art.

EXPERIMENTAL
DEFAULT
ABSTRACT
CONCEPTUAL
UNWEARABLE

KIM
IAAH
BURBUSH DESIGN
HOLZINGER
TONG
KNIFE KNIFE
JUAN VG
MATLAKAS
LOBEBALL STUDIO
T-BOT
LEHMANN

66

061 — SAN KIM — KOR — THE BLOW UP

The inflatables created by the designer during the pandemic were his interpretation of how society was responding to the virus. As he searched the Internet, he would often find images of people cautiously peering out with supermarket plastic bags over their heads while on the subway (due to a shortage of masks). These images made him sympathetic towards the people and also gave him a boost of positive energy since they were not using plastic bags for trash— they were being creative. Photographed by Kerry J Dean. ↪ see also p. 69

061 ↦ see p. 67

064—SOLEDAD GALLARDO / BURBUSH DESIGN—ESP—WEARABLE TYPOGRAPHY

"What would happen if I transformed letters into wearables?" This question lingered in Soledad's mind the day she learned about the 36 Days of Type challenge. There was only one way to answer it, so she decided to bring it to life—digitally.

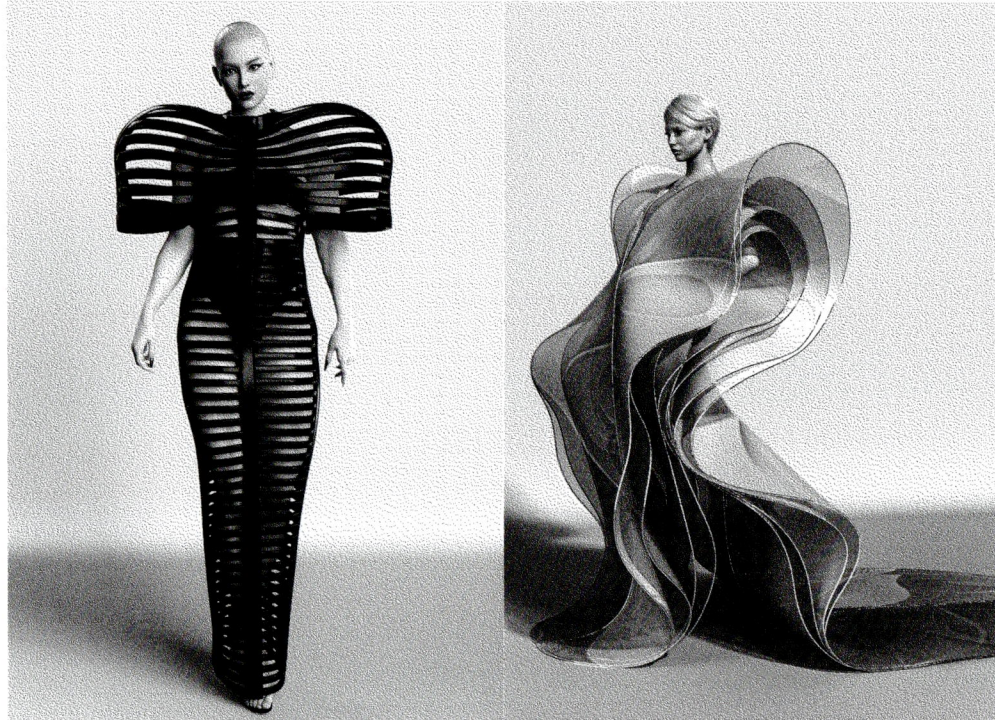

065—LUCA HOLZINGER—FRA—TRESPASSERS WILL BE FORGIVEN

The collection is an ode to the designer's interest in architecture which was initially triggered by his father. The artist Gordon Matta-Clark is the main inspiration. He did interventions on old existing buildings and created something new with the simple action of cutting. Holzinger translated this idea in his garments by slicing, turning, and perforating. The type of person he want to portray is a reference to the person of Matta-Clark who went beyond barricades to create something beautiful. Collection by Luca Holzinger, Graphic Design by Janic Fotsch, Campaign Shoot by Vital Romero, and Model is Donald Huycke

066—XIXI TONG AND KNIFE KNIFE—GBR—HILDR (BATTLE). LOOK 1 OF THE FUTURE VALKYRIES COLLECTION
People are increasingly entrusting the future to the virtual world, but the real world is still ravaged by war and injustice, with women's rights in regression. It's time to shift our attention back to the world around us, to pick up our spears in this never-ending battle for equality and liberation. The dress incorporates excerpts from *Wið færstice* and *For a Swarm of Bees*—two charms that describe valkyries. Garment design by Xixi Tong; variable typeface SPEARS by Knife Knife.

067—JUAN VALENTIN-GAMAZO / JUAN VG—ESP—GAMBERRXS

JUAN VG is not just a brand, it's a statement. It's for those who dare to stand out, who embrace their individuality with pride. These pieces are a expressions of freedom, creativity, and rebellion. From edgy hand-painted designs to bold airbrush creations, each garment tells a story of defiance and authenticity. Born in Valladolid, the designs draw inspiration from the raw energy of the grunge scene in contrast to the Spanish "pijo" style, creating a style that is both distinctive and daring. Creative direction by Juan VG. Production by Juan VG and Santiago Neyra. Photography coordination by Santiago Neyra. Photography by Anna Mendiola and Irene Golvano. Jewelry by Vanina Palmeto. Make-up and hair design by Laura del Muro, sponsored by Icon Spain and Termix. Stylist assistants include Fatima Miñana, Raul Gonzalez, and Paco Platero. Make-up and hair assistants include Julia Cadia and Mattioni.

HUMAN TYPER is a performance art piece where the artist, adorned with alphabet stamps, prints letters onto a large sheet, reflecting on the world's pace. It's a deliberate act, slowing down to ponder each letter's significance, contrasting our fast-paced, tech-driven society. The audience engages, suggesting words, adding to the narrative. This tactile communication emphasizes the effort behind each letter, fostering a deeper connection with our messages.

069—LESLEY DILL / LESLEY DILL STUDIO—USA—HELL HELL HELL / HEAVEN HEAVEN HEAVEN : ENCOUNTERING SISTER GERTRUDE MORGAN AND REVELATION

This installation is the story of Dill's encounter with Sister Gertrude and the Book of Revelations. Sister Gertrude Morgan was a preacher, artist, musician and poet who worked in New Orleans in the 1960's and 1970's. Morgan was primarily noted for her folk art. She had a vision that she was to commit her life to Christ, and she was to wear only white as she was now the Bride of Jesus. Brightly colored fabric words, Glory, Power, Revelation, etc. are hand sewn onto the white dress.

070——HAILEE TALBOT
——USA——
IS FASHION IS RELIGION IS

In her research, Hailee Talbot grapples with the similarities of Haute Couture and Catholicism, and their connection to graphic design through harmony, balance, and rhythm. This garment is a manifestation of that research with a circle skirt reading: "FASHION IS RELIGION IS," with the intention of it being read as both, "FASHION IS RELIGION" and "RELIGION IS FASHION." The capelet, headpiece, and fabric colors are signifiers of various Catholic regalia.

071—LESLEY DILL / LESLEY DILL STUDIO—USA—WHITE HINGED POEM DRESS

What has kept Lesley Dill inspired by Emily Dickinson's words? Dill is inspired by this small woman writing about huge, tremendous ideas ("This World is not conclusion—a species stands beyond—invisible as Music—but positive as Sound") even as she evokes the smallest details of life around her, with nuanced, tiny emotions that whiplash about ("The Soul has Bandaged moments") or settle into a deep peace ("To be alive is Power—existence in itself—without a further function —Omnipotence enough"). Two words come to Dill's mind in thinking of her work: Poignancy + Force. Together, this mix of beauty and edge in her words, is what they carry from her into their art works—the vulnerability, the power, the darkness, the yearning for an inner ecstatic feeling: "Some too fragile for winter winds," "I took my Power in my hand and went against the world."

072—LESLEY DILL / LESLEY DILL STUDIO—USA—WORD QUEEN OF LAUGHTER

Lesley Dill loved creating a dress where opening a flap would reveal a phrase. Together, all these sections formed a poem within the dress. The text used was from *You May Laugh …* by Salvador Espriu:

"You May Laugh
but I feel within Me suddenly
Strange Voices of god and Handles
Dog's thirst and message of Slow Memories
that Disappear
Across a Fragile Bridge"

073—PABLO LEHMANN—ARG—CORTAZAR'S SHIRT

Lehmann feels strongly attracted to words, and always wonders how much language constitutes our reality. In the last twenty years he has explored written texts in metaphorical and aesthetic dimensions, in order to present language as a material object, embodied in our lives. Using the cut-out technique, his works invites the reader to unpredictable text discoveries. His work CORTAZAR'S SHIRT belong to the series *Attires,* in which he created clothes using fragments of texts of writers.

TYPOGRAPHY

The black shirt with the yellow Nirvana logo is now available at H&M, in soft pink, with glitter text. It's the favorite shirt of our colleague's 8-year-old daughter. A sort of typographic socialization. A consciousness-expanding process showing that typography and fashion do indeed go together.

ABC
GLYPHS
FONTS
NUMBERS
LETTERS

PIERCY
BEIRENDONCK
KD26 A
PRODUCTION TYPE
HANSEL GROTESQUE STUDIO
APPEAR OFFLINE
SKIP
KÖNIG
DIER
PUBLIC POSSESSION
BUREAU BORSCHE
CASALI
ČESKA
PS TYPE
CARLONI
BEIERARBEIT
I'D KNIT THAT
HAIDER
40MUSTAQEL
KHOMENKO
SCHULTE KELLINGHAUS
KRAFT
MAYER
HWANG
INFORMAL PROJECT
WAGNER
KÖNIGSTEIN
STAJCZAK

074—ANNA PIERCY—GBR—A-DRESS

This style was shown at Graduate Fashion Week 2010, and was part of a collection based on a vintage Scrabble board Anna's parents had had since she before she was born. Each piece was a letter and together they spelled "RANDOM." Using the color palette and prints inspired from the Scrabble board, each piece of the collection was made from sculptural neoprene, fused wool mixed or soft silk jersey. Photographed by Hugh O'Malley.

076—KD26 A—NLD—KD26 A

KD26 A is a handmade kimono, designed and created by fashion designer Korinna van Balkom and graphic designer Daan Rietbergen. A unique, typographic artwork made from a upcycled 100% wool blanket in which the lowercase letter "a" is integrated. Accompanied by a grid, the shape of the letter moves repetitively from right to left. This makes the structured shape dynamic. The grid and movement are integrated into the kimono by using an enlarged and self-developed "tufting technique."

077—JEAN-BAPTISTE LEVÉE / PRODUCTION TYPE—FRA—DEUS EX MACHINA "PIPES" APPAREL AND "PLENTY" COACH JACKET

The T-shirt titled *Pipes* features the typeface *Cardinal Fruit,* a sub-family in the larger *Cardinal* collection designed and published by Production Type under the guidance of Jean-Baptiste Levée. The jacket named *Plenty* is from the Deus Customs series. Its highlights are purely typographic and feature *Brush Script*, an American classic from the 1940s, and *Enfantine*, a script typeface designed by Jean-Baptiste Levée from Production Type.

078—HANSEL GROTESQUE STUDIO—ITA—JACQUARD BLANKETS

Produced only on demand and with close to zero production waste, Viceversa is a 100 % percent merino wool jacquard blanket, made in the workshop of Lanificio Leo in Southern Italy. Initially conceived in grey and black, it was later included in the company's catalog by owner Emilio Leo, with whom we took the decision of adding the color combinations red and turquoise, and purple and green. Its design, centered on the graphic reversibility of fabrics, is the work of London-based designer Gianluca Alla. Manufacture: Lanificio Leo, Models: Gaia Carnevale, Francesco Bigatti, Midori Ogihara, Emanuele Abbondanza. Clothes: Ascend Beyond. Stylist: Emanuele Abbondanza. Photography: Michela Pedranti. Courtesy: Hansel Grotesque Studio

079—APPEAR OFFLINE—HRV—VIVID DREAMS SHIRT

VIVID DREAMS is a custom-made shirt that captures the essence of artistic expression and personal style. This garment features short sleeves and an all-over print, crafted from 100% viscose at 120 grams. The design highlights a captivating contrast between textured and distorted graphics, creating an engaging visual effect that aligns with the sleek, custom fit. This seamless fusion of patterns and materials elevates the shirt from a basic item to a unique and memorable fashion piece.

080——SERGEY SKIP——
DEU——CONTROL / CONSUME

A collaboration between visual artist Sergey Skip and Berlin-based fashion brand FUENF. Garments are used as a canvas for chaos. Adorned with fragmented and broken type, they are embracing the beauty in imperfection.

Eike König designed a football shirt commissioned by Hen's Teeth, as well as a soccer ball commissioned by Pupilla for an exhibition. He added a personal touch by including his son's name on the shirt, creating a unique jersey just for him.

082——LISELOTTE
——DEU

DIER
——MDNSS

MDNSS is all about giving new life to old clothes, hiding in the back of the closet that seem too boring for daily usage. Inspired by the chaos of modern life and overstimulating expectations, MDNSS slows down the fashion world by handmade screen printing, creating unique patterns and special pieces. The slow process hopes to bring a bit of calm to our fast-paced society and revive the appreciation for single pieces, while protesting the madness of the world.

083—PUBLIC POSSESSION—DEU—GRAPHIC SHIRTS

Various T-Shirt designs by Public Possession, founded in 2012 by Valentino Betz and Marvin Schuhmann as an outlet to channel their various interests. The idea of the studio is to emphasize the relationship between music, text, graphic design and happenings. All Label / Apparel related artwork and public relations are done inhouse.

085—BUREAU BORSCHE—DEU—SUPREME
SUPREME Gradient Jacquard Jacket, designed by Leonhard Laupichler, 2022.

086—VALENTINA CASALI—ITA—BELIEVE ↙
Do you believe in ghosts? Do you believe in magic? Do you believe in miracles? Do you believe in yourself? Adapting to strange times seems to be the only way to survive in these uncertain times, being fluid and in motion, pivoting through difficulties, and remaining hopeful under a warm and soft blanket.

087—VALENTINA CASALI—ITA—DEATH ↘
Two colors hand punched mini-rug / banner as part of the Tiger-Mochi collection. This specimen is unique: it's sewn and assembled by hand. Dimension: 26.5 cm × 26.5 cm wool threads punched on sewing canvas, with gray felt underneath, finished by hand.

088—ANNIJA ČESKA—AUT—GO WITH THE FLOW ↖
Lettering for a bucket hat.

089—MARK CANESO / PS TYPE—USA—TYPEFACE COVER ↗
This bandana was created as a symbol of optimism about the future. At a time when masks were essential to everyday life, its design reflected hope for a time when they would no longer be needed. The bandana was intended to have a life beyond the pandemic, with versatility that allowed it to be worn over the face, around the neck, on the head, or simply displayed as art on the wall.

090——SOPHIA CARLONI——DEU—— DIY-IDENTITY KIT

Fashion serves as a means of expressing one's identity. It acts as a subtle form of communication, carrying one's self-image into the public sphere. The DIY-IDENTITY KIT allows each individual to design and customize unique typographic fashion pieces through stencils, providing the opportunity for flexible expression of one's identity. In contrast to pre-made fashion that follows specific trends, the KIT enables the authentic representation of personal preferences and expressions.

091—MARK CANESO / PS TYPE—USA—FOOTNOTES
Going "All Knit, No Quit" on these custom crew socks made for the designer who knows that (point) size matters.

092—BEIERARBEIT—DEU—FESTIVAL FÜR NEUE MUSIK
The Festival for New Music is a two-day event at the Konzerthaus Bielefeld for the free interpretation of classical music in the transition to improvisation and experimentation. New shoes for new paths. The somewhat differently staged admission ticket in the form of a Typo Chuck for a "meet & greet" behind the scenes.

093— KENDALL ROSS / I'D KNIT THAT BIG —USA— FEELINGS

Big vest, hand-knit with wool. 4' × 4', 2024.

I get bored and decide it's time to up and cry get worked about things that never mattered to me 'til I found out there's a way it was supposed to be. And you get to see all my insecurities—I go off and complain publicly about all of the wrong you did to me like it's just what I've always believed and not a reaction to all your rejection. Do I even value your opinion? Or do I just crave the opposition? It's an obsession, I can't make anything without your voice in my head

094—LUKAS HAIDER—AUT—365 DAYS OF TAU ↓
One year anniversary T-shirt design for the German record label TAU, using a beta version of Haider's custom typeface *UNKNOWN*.

095—40MUSTAQEL—EGY—RIZO MASR ↑
RIZO MASR is a risograph printing service based in Cairo. 40MUSTAQEL was tasked with the visual identity and branding for the studio. The name, translating to "Rizo Egypt," draws from the typical style of company names in Nasserist Egypt and the nationalization of foreign companies at the time, adjacent to the introduction of the risograph printing technology in Japan. The typography is inspired by the style prevalent in cinema posters and TV title cards during that era.

096—VOLODYMYR KHOMENKO—UKR—KUNSTKAMMER

Merchandise inspired by THE KUNSTKAMMER and its collection of fantastical creatures. This collection of merchandise tells a captivating story of THE KUNSTKAMMER, a museum of natural history and curiosities. Among these creatures are a mischievous medieval jester, mythical birds from ancient lore, and fierce wild boars. The organic and sinuous forms of these creatures stand in stark contrast to the geometric precision of Ziggurat, a modular custom font designed for this collection.

097—LUIS SCHULTE KELLINGHAUS, ANNE KRAFT, JAKOB MAYER—DEU—A JERSEY FOR ABK STUTTGART
The new jersey for Stuttgart Art Academy's football club was designed using a fully typographic approach. A white jersey, custom letterings, and numbers form the teams identity.

029—SEE P. 32

098—DAHYUN HWANG—DEU—CARHARTT WIP KUALA LUMPUR STORE OPENING T-SHIRT
To celebrate the opening of Carhartt WIP Kuala Lumpur TRX in January 2024, a set of limited editions was designed, including a T-shirt and a sweatshirt. Both items feature a reworked Carhartt WIP "C" logo and graphic artwork using typography and abstract elements.

100—VINCENT WAGNER—AUT—TEMPORARY HARDWARE ↓
TEMPORARY HARDWARE is a series of 3D printed typographic fashion accessories. Overall shapes and functional parts are based solely on typographic elements. The chokers shown here are the first in-progress test for the series, which is intended to include rings, bracelets, necklaces, and other accessories.

101—JUDITH KÖNIGSTEIN—DEU—MOVABLE GRAPHIC PIN ↑
This movable graphic pin is meant to be combined with any type of clothing and accessory. It can visually enhance basic pieces and add an individual expression to them.

102 — NATALIA RATAJCZAK
POL — 3D PRINTED EARRINGS

These 3D-printed earrings were designed to explore calligraphy-inspired forms, bridging abstraction with typography and fashion. The calligraphic ornaments were initially created using a broad nib pen and ink. The designs were then digitized and transformed into 3D objects, which were subsequently sliced and printed on a Prusa 3D printer.

MINIMAL

We all remember the impact of a small crocodile on a white polo shirt worn by the popper (Lacoste) versus the black BOSS shirts (Hugo Boss) worn by the tough guy. Minimalism is the art of modesty. But what brand truly wants that? To be modest?

REDUCED
SMALL
SHARP
PRECISE
SWISS

KLOTZ
STUDIO 5115 SNC
VOLKART
STAFFORD
ORTNER ETC.
ARBUZOV
STUDIO KATRAHMANI
TAMTI
MEHNER
TUCCI
BROECKER
HERMES
AGOF
RUTZ
JESCHINA

103—VIKTORIA KLOTZ—DEU—STAINS IN A ROW
T-Shirt collection which literally plays with stains we get on shirts. This work was created at the Faculty of Design Darmstadt.

104— SCHNEEBERGER 5115 SNC—CHE— / ROBERTO STUDIO 5115 CAP

Series of ready-to-wear and accessories blending a minimal aesthetic designed by Studio 5115.
Components:
100 % originality +
50 % creativity +
50 % dyslexia
----
200 % Studio 5115

105—LOÏC VOLKART—CHE—QUE DES NUMÉROS 10

Don't produce new jerseys. Print empty! Urgent creation of football jerseys without consequences. Choose the remaining sports equipment in a second-hand store. Multiple cuts and colors. Zico, Zidane, Bergkamp … be a number 10! Cut out and stick the numbers 10 on the back of the jerseys. Print an entire silkscreen frame in vibrant green. No need to attach content, just stamp empty. Remove the stencil. The number 10 fades away, revealing the original fabric. The rectangle creates unity.

These text works were made through an experimental process, including plaster castings, embossing, and collage. Utilizing texture and light primarily, words, against the prompt of FASHION, try to make themselves visible in playful arrangements.

107——ORTNER ETC.——
AUT—— 10 JAHRE AREA®

Design for the work jacket celebrating the 10th anniversary of the furniture design store AREA®.

108——ORTNER
ETC.——AUT——22K

Merch, jersey, and label design for the restaurant 22K.

109—MAKSIM ARBUZOV—MNE—READY 4 WHATEVER

The contemporary sportswear brand Barboza has taken the initiative to produce a unique typography print for each new collection. Embracing the motto READY 4 WHATEVER, the brand sought to incorporate it as a central print theme. Maksim Arbuzov was honored to be commissioned to design this distinctive print, capturing the essence of Barboza's technological spirit.

110—GOLNAR KAT-RAHMANI / STUDIO GOLNAR KATRAHMANI—DEU—NAMAK-E SAFAR (THE TASTE OF THE JOURNEY)

The fashion collection NAMAK-E SAFAR (The Taste of the Journey) talks about the distances and made to support the project TYPE & POLITICS – DEPOLITICIZING ARABIC LETTERS. For joining different worlds based on a mutual interest in typography. The designs on display make use of square Kofic letters – in Persian, limited editions in silkscreen, by G.Kat.Berlin. They show the names of Middle Eastern cities, where the Arabic alphabet is originated & their distances in kilometers to Berlin.

Type Fashion 119 Slanted #44

111—ORTNER ETC.—AUT—COPYRIGHT BY STEIERMARK ↓
Coat design for the pop-up store COPYRIGHT BY STEIERMARK, the intellectual property of Styrian winemakers from the winegrowing regions of Styria. Photography by Florian Voggeneder.

112—CIHAN TAMTI—DEU—CALVIN KLEIN ↑
Cihan Tamti was hired as a special talent to design graphic concepts for Calvin Klein's main line. The goal was to bring Calvin Klein's heritage back to the forefront of their customers' minds while representing New York. Additionally, he designed logo iterations.

113—JOHANNA MEHNER—DEU—UGLY CUTE

UGLY CUTE is exaggerated in every way: this typeface is wider, more important, better and worse than it has any right to be. UGLY CUTE is fantastic, it's annoying, it's flamboyant, it is queer. The UGLY CUTE Jacket is this typeface come to life—blown up, with extreme proportions. A hand-sewn quilted jacket in contrasting, gaudy colors. Huge sleeves, ultra cropped, and a collar standing so tall, it swallows its wearer up to the eyes. This ugly cute jacket is one of the most eye-catching pick-me pieces.

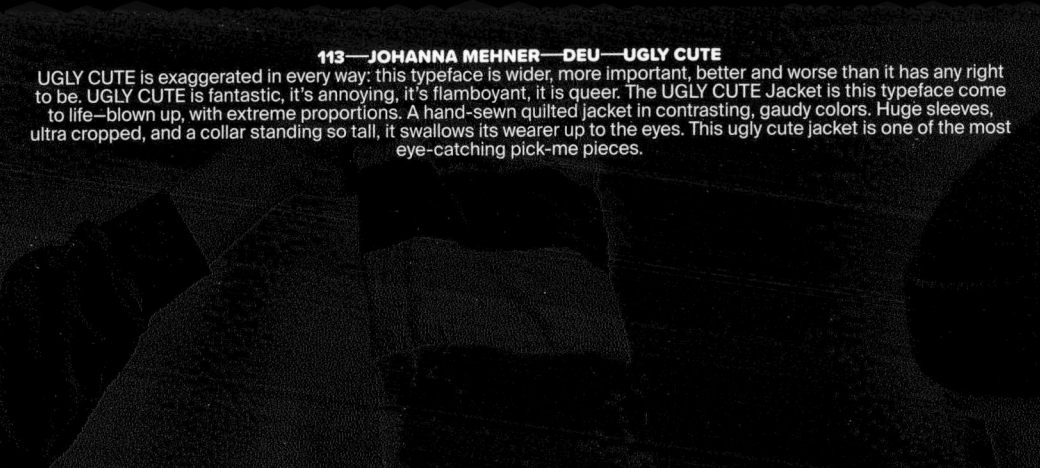

114——GIANPAOLO TUCCI——
DEU——ATELIER ABOUT

Atelier About, led by directors Gianpaolo Tucci and Giulio D'Alessio, showcases the collections *TERROR(ism)* (displayed on the left side and upper right side) and *CENSORSHIP* (featured on the bottom right side). The photography is the work of Pernille Sandberg and Sandra Ebert, with models Julian Zacharias Eide, Zoe Jungbluth, and Daniel Krone.

VALUE is a collection of leather bags and upcycled shirts, combining conscious design with AI-aided visual exploration and traditional craftsmanship. To ensure resource-saving manufacture, discarded leather furniture and secondhand textiles were used. Written "warning labels" accompany each bag, giving instructions on how to interact with and experience them—opening a space inbetween usable object and abstract sculpture aiming to question the value perception of everyday objects.

116—ALENA HERMES—DEU—I AM THE REASON

This metamorphosis of a recycled second-hand blazer into a two-piece outfit is intended to encourage self-reflection. Its message—to take responsibility for our environment, particularly in relation to wildfires. The text on the back of the top is a reminder—we must be aware of the impact of our actions; the text on the front of the skirt gives advice on how to reduce wildfires, highlighting methods for improvement. The clothes incorporate burnt areas to draw attention to the theme. This work is part of the *Words Clothes Expression* project by Klasse Roberts at ABK Stuttgart.
↦ see also p. 127

> IT IS IMPORTANT TO ADDRESS THE VARIOUS FACTORS THAT CONTRIBUTE TO FOREST FIRES IN DIFFERENT REGIONS AND TO WORK TOWARDS PREVENTING AND MITIGATING THEIR IMPACT THROUGH A COMBINATION OF EDUCATION, AWARENESS CAMPAIGNS, REGULATION, AND INVESTMENT IN FIRE PREVENTION AND FIREFIGHTING INFRASTRUCTURE.

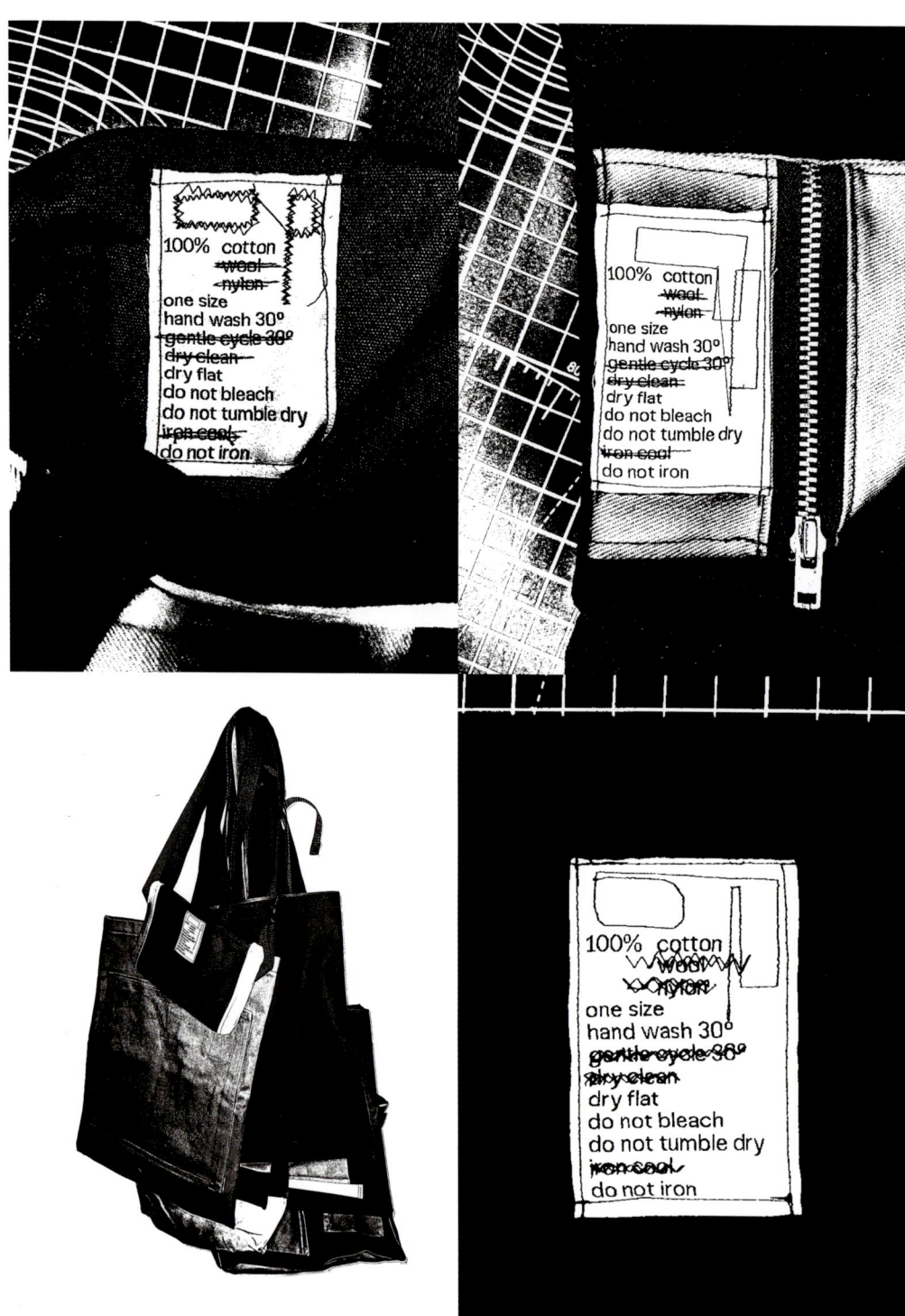

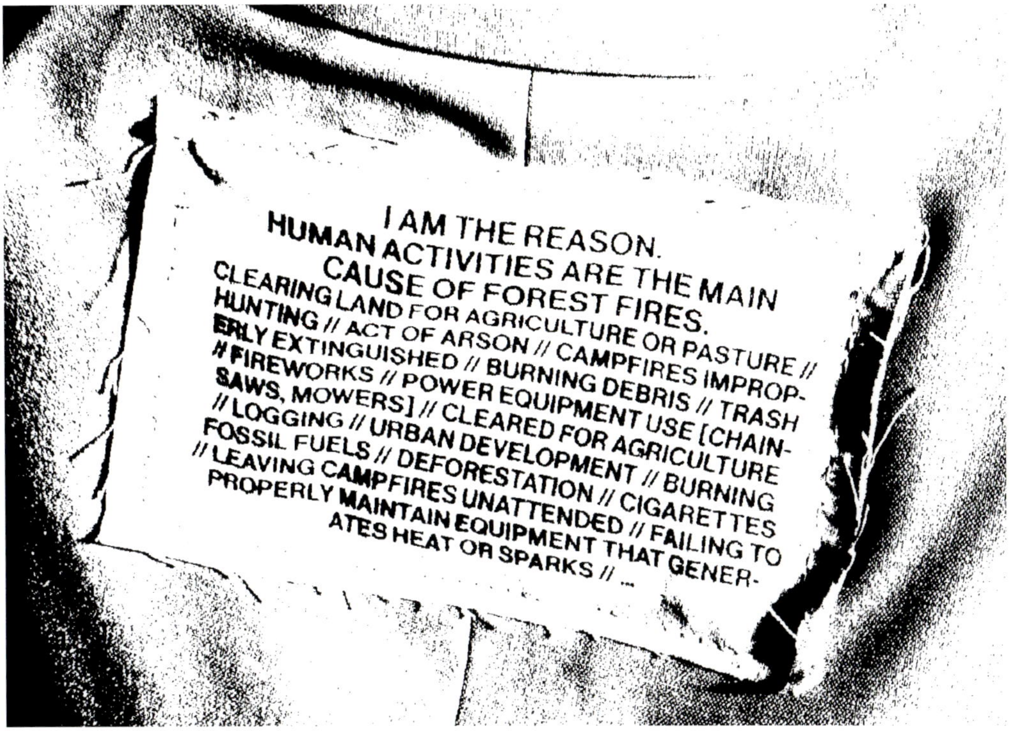

118—LUIS RUTZ—DEU—55555 ON SILK

55555 is not a typeface, but a structuring machine! This open modular system uses the unicode classification order to turn a simple font file into a controlling tool for all visual applications. Based on a simple 5 × 5 grid, it provides more than 400 glyphs for Latin and Cyrillic script, plus numerous graphical elements, wildly combinable in an almost infinite manner. Layered on silk, digital repetition, and haptic sensation. It is the first in a series of wearable pieces.

119—CHARLOTTE JESCHINA—DEU—GRWM

GRWM is short for "get ready with me." It is a series of a text, which is layouted as the parts of an outfit described in it and then layered to shape the wearer. The content, as well as the presentation, is a play on the interaction of clothes and their wearers. The parts work both as a series and individually (except for the plain text).

I'm
an
empty
shape
in front
of a war
drobe
. Rea
dy to
b
e
s
o
m
e
th i
n
g

first, there is the underwear with pumapumapumapuma written on it

next, i need to chose, who i am today. and I want to be f-e-m-m-e, so I pick a dress. it is l⌐ng and flowy and black with small white dots on it. sophis ticated, witchy, who is she? not me, y e t, I think.

the sweater I wear ov er it is knit ed in green cab les th ey say it ma kes my eyes pop. b ut it makes me feel pa le,

... so I take off the sweater I wear ov er it is knit ed in green cab les

because April i s cold here and i am always cold in April, I layer a jacket of denim, that is not really mine. it will h ang lose on the empty shape th at is now beco ming me but wi ll keep me warm in Ap ril cold li ke the hug of the per son wh o's denim jacket I w ear.

and put on a black shirt of heavy cotton. screenprinted with the name of a band I like. BOSTON MANOR is what it now proclaims and I think of a song that is dedicated to nobody and dedicate my fit to them.

almost, I think, while adding a belt for shape

next a necklace, that loopsloopsloopsloops around my neck

Then, I put on a smile.

the b oots with the do c martens bouncy sole s tag on the back, I put on last. though they have not been least since I was sixteen. I wear them with socks and lace them upupupupu pupup to the top.

TYPEFACES

Fashion brands have understood: to make a difference, you must stand out. An unmistakable typeface is a part of the value chain. In the constant cycle of collections, identity-giving stability is needed. No other design element can do better than corporate type.

EXCLUSIVE IN USE CUSTOM CORPORATE SPECIAL

STUDIO FABIO BIESEL
DISPLAAY
SYLVAIN
LATINOTYPE
SCHICK TOIKKA
PRODUCTION TYPE
YOTAFONTS
205TF
29LETTERS TYPE FOUNDRY [29LT]
HARDAL STUDIO

120—STUDIO FABIO BIESEL—DEU—GÜGGELI & INCREASE FOR ACNE STUDIOS

For Fabio Biesel it was incredibly exciting that his typefaces *Güggeli* and *Increase* were selected by Acne Studios for their *Akcne Stadyums Stoketown 13* collection. The key design goal was to create a surprising effect by intentionally exaggerating and mixing already wild typefaces. This approach resulted in a fresh, artistic look that permeates the entire collection.

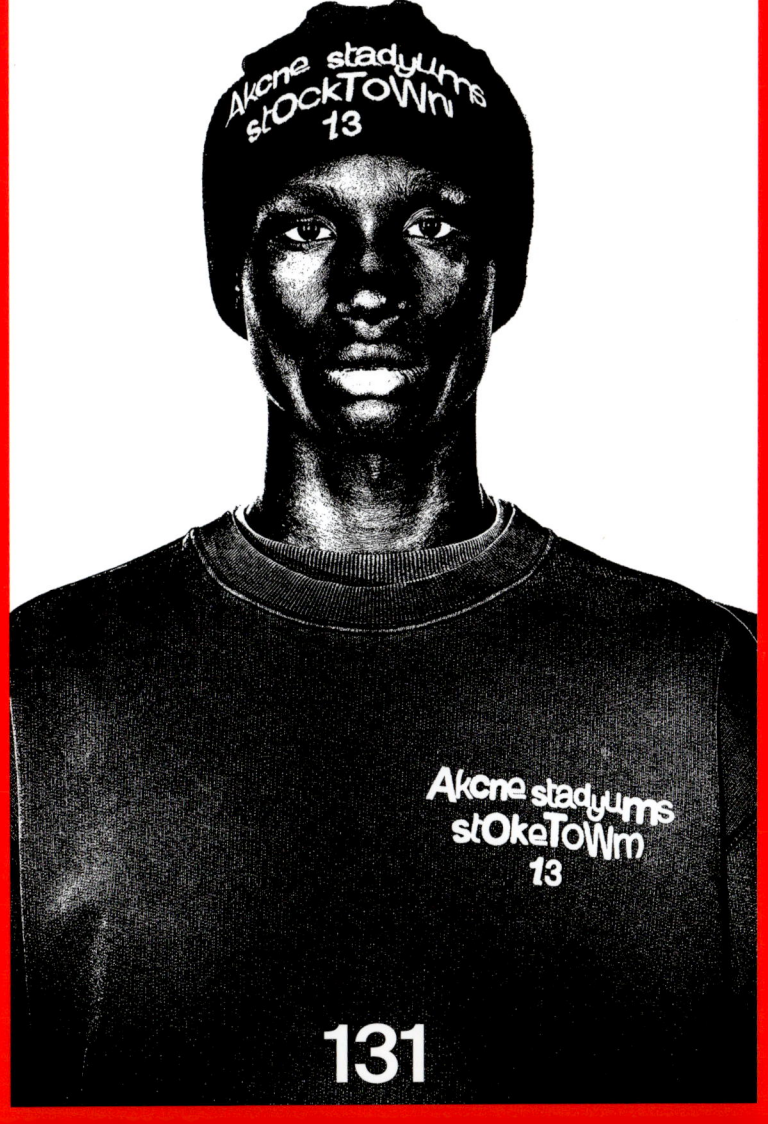

122—LATINOTYPE—CHL—LA PLAGE

LA PLAGE (French "the beach"), is a unique French Concept Store created by a Chilean-French couple Gaby and Ben. It features exclusive garments and objects from international designers (such as Obey, Piet Parra and Felipe Pantone), alongside emerging independent Chilean brands. The project is a rebranding. Latinotype developed an urban, eclectic, and friendly font identity system for consistent use across all graphic and visual supports. They used the number of letters in "Plage" as a reference, defining a concept for each weight: five concepts, five weights. Creative direction by Dany Berczeller, Daniel Hernández, and Luciano Vergara. Art direction by Nicolas Tobar, Ignacio Sekul, and Dany Berczeller. Type design by César Araya and Alfonso García and photographed by Carlos Molina.

123—JEAN-BAPTISTE LEVÉE / PRODUCTION TYPE—FRA—CARHARTT WORK IN PROGRESS (WIP)

Signal typeface by Production Type in use by CARHARTT WIP. *Signal Compressed* is the extra compressed style, skewed and excessive, wittily rounding out the *Signal* family. It carries a complete set of accents for multilingual typesetting, numerous arrows and pictograms, and characters for mathematical typesetting.

124—JEAN-BAPTISTE LEVÉE / PRODUCTION TYPE—FRA—COURRÈGES

Courrèges is the exclusive typeface designed for the COURRÈGES fashion brand. The *Courrèges* typeface is a plain, pointy sans that serves as a multipurpose companion to the new logotype by art director Jean-Baptiste Talbourdet. The type takes its cues from archetypical designs such as *Futura* and *Erbar*, emblematic of the German geometric style from the first half of the 20th century. The single-weight typeface works across the ready-to-wear and eyewear collections, as well as the COURRÈGES boutique network. Client: Courrèges, 2016; Art direction: Jean-Baptiste Talbourdet, Lolita Jacobs.

125—SCHICK TOIKKA—DEU / FIN—MARI SANS & MARI SLAB FOR MARIMEKKO

Founded in 1951, Marimekko is a Finnish design company renowned for its original prints and colors. For their rebranding, Schick Toikka created a custom typeface that comes in Sans and Slab variants, including an extensive set of figures and symbols. The design is based on the iconic Marimekko logotype which has its roots in the Olivetti typewriter letters favored by founder Armi Ratia. Art direction by Tsto. Images courtesy of Marimekko.

Isot Kivet
●●●●●

STANDARD 100
by OEKO-TEX®
100% Cotton

Colors: Black & White
$34.78 / repeat (23 in)
Color ID: 001

Maija Louekari
Fujiwo Ishimoto
Ristomatti Ratia
Katsuji Wakisaka
Annika Rimala
Maija Isola

Unikko ❀
"Poppy"

Pieni Unikko 2
Cotton Fabric
49,00 € / m

Colors: beige, d.green &
white. Repeat = length
of pattern: 88 cm

136

Slanted #44   Type Fashion

NIKE UNLACED FOR NIKE UNLACED

NIKE UNLACED is a global digital and retail concept, defining Nike's new women's sneaker boutique launched in Paris during fashion week in spring 2018. Together with design studio Deutsche & Japaner, Schick Toikka created a typeface relating to the idea of twisted laces. Creative direction: Maria Vu, Project manager: Miko Cowan, Art Direction: Deutsche & Japaner, Space design: Robert Storey / Storey Studio, Space build: Satis & Fy, Product photography: Leandro Farino. Images courtesy of Nike.

127 — TYPE LV LOUIS — CLÉMENCE VUITTON — PRODUCTION FRA FOR MAGAZINE

Louis Vuitton wanted to publish a first-class consumer magazine while maintaining its leadership position in global fashion design. *LV Clémence* showcases the complexity of an inherited brand that knows how to stay modern, turning its magazine into a sophisticated publication whose visual appearance is up to the demands of such an expansive label. Client: Louis Vuitton; Art Direction: Yorgo Tloupas, Yorgo & Co.

128—YOTAFONTS—FRA—HAPPY FONT & HAPPY SCRIPT

For their rebranding of Happy Socks, the Yotafonts team designed two typefaces made to match. The first one is a Sans Serif family with concave stems (reminiscent of the smiling "H" logo they also designed), which includes one style for headlines, and three styles for texts. The second one, a Sans Serif, is paired with a very low contrast script typeface. The style of this script typeface is inspired by the numerous letterings of shops, hotels, and restaurants signs, typical of the streets of Stockholm.

129—205TF—FRA—EXPOSURE FOR GRANNY
Typeface *Exposure* by 205TF, designed by Federico Parra Barrois, with graphic design by Patrick Fry Studio (2024).

130 — 205TF
FRA MOLITOR QUINTA
FOR MASO

Typeface *Molitor* by 205TF, designed by Matthieu Cortat for Quinta Maso, with graphic design by Paula Maso (2021).

131—29LETTERS TYPE FOUNDRY [29LT]—ESP—CUSTOM ARABIC LOGOTYPE FOR LANVIN
In the Arab world, shop signs often feature both Arabic and Western scripts. For Lanvin, the French fashion house, a new logotype was introduced in 2022 with a modern serif typography. Pascal Zoghbi was tasked with designing the Arabic logotype to complement this. He explored two Arabic calligraphic styles—Thuluth and Eastern Kufic—both high in contrast to match the Latin design. The final Arabic logotype integrated elements like a distinctive Lam-Alef combination and diamond-shaped diacritic dots, reflecting the sharp modernity of the Western script.

132—29LETTERS TYPE FOUNDRY [29LT] —ESP—CUSTOM ARABIC LOGOTYPE FOR BALENCIAGA

In 2017, Balenciaga revamped its brand identity, adopting a sleek, condensed sans serif type. In 2019, Pascal Zoghbi was tasked with designing an Arabic logotype to match this new identity. He opted for a simplified Kufic style, aligning the Arabic baseline and heights with the Latin type while incorporating straight terminals and rectangular diacritic dots. The final design maintains a block-like structure, reflecting the modernity of the Latin logo while accommodating Arabic script characteristics.

133—HARDAL STUDIO—TUR—ALKAZAR TYPEFACE

HOPE Alkazar is a platform by Nike, uniting communities through sports, culture, and art, centered on social good. It's a stage for innovation and diversity, connecting people from Asia and Europe in Istanbul's Beyoğlu. HOPE Alkazar inspires new perspectives for a better future.

HOPE Alkazar

Light — HIIT
Regular — DANCE
Medium — INTERVIEW
Semi-Bold — WORKSHOP
Bold — CINEMA

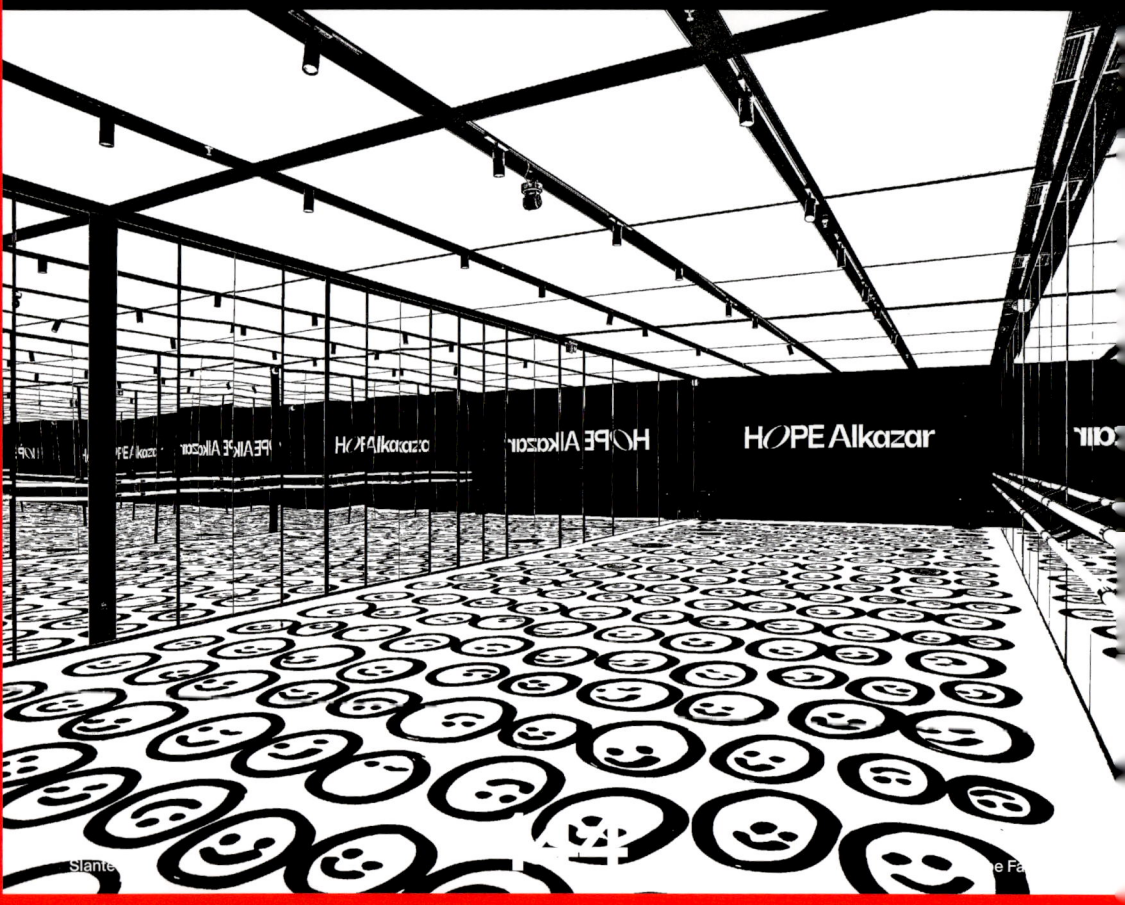

QUENTINO

stay true to yourself

hks-farben.de

HKS

FREREJONES.COM

SUPERMASSIVE

Airflow
Sojourner
Monocle
Relocate
Quicker
Multiples

Adjunct
processtype.com

ST Brel
ST Dani
ST Guust

ST KdG
ST Lungta
ST Toone
ST Toone Sans
ST Elegant
ST Tenzin
ST Wiels

new fonts
with a Belgian twist

exclusively available
at studiotype.be

Fairgates Extra Light
Fairgates Light
Fairgates Normal
Fairgates Medium
Fairgates Semi Bold
Fairgates Bold
Fairgates Extra Bold

Fairgates Extra Light Italic
Fairgates Light Italic
Fairgates Normal Italic
Fairgates Medium Italic
Fairgates Semi Bold Italic
Fairgates Bold Italic
Fairgates Extra Bold Italic

www.norbergtypefoundry.com

 This is Fairgates from Norberg Type Foundry, available in seven weights and as a variable font

180 typefaces

YEAR-BOOK OF TYPE

Squeezed ... Thin ... Squeezed Light, Squeezed Light Italic, Squeezed Medium, Squeezed Medium Italic, Squeezed Dark, Squeezed Dark Italic, Squeezed Dense, Squeezed Dense Italic, Condensed Fine, Condensed Fine Italic, Condensed Regular, Condensed Italic, Condensed Bold, Condensed Bold Italic, Condensed Black, Condensed Black Italic, Tight Thin, Tight Thin Italic, Tight Light, Tight Light Italic, Tight Medium, Tight Medium Italic, Tight Dark, Tight Dark Italic, Tight Dense, Tight Dense Italic, Narrow Fine, Narrow Fine Italic, Narrow Regular, Narrow Italic, Narrow Bold, Narrow Bold Italic, Narrow Black, Narrow Black Italic, Compact Thin, Compact Thin Italic, Compact Light, Compact Light Italic, Compact Medium, Compact Medium Italic, Compact Dark, Compact Dark Italic, Compact Dense, Compact Dense Italic, Fine, Fine Italic, Regular, Italic, Bold, Bold Italic, Black, Black Italic, Ample Thin, Ample Thin Italic, Ample Light, Ample Light Italic, Ample Medium, Ample Medium Italic, Ample Dark, Ample Dark Italic, Ample Dense, Ample Dense Italic, Wide Fine, Wide Fine Italic, Wide Regular, Wide Italic, Wide Bold, Wide Bold Italic, Wide Black, Wide Black Italic, Grand Thin, Grand Thin Italic, Grand Light, Grand Light Italic, Grand Medium, Grand Medium Italic, Grand Dark, Grand Dark Italic, Grand Dense, Grand Dense Italic

№ 7 ↓ *Coming Nov. '24*

The Yearbook of Type is a collection of the latest published typefaces and helps to find the one—from a browse through the book, or quick look in the index that neatly sorts typefaces by names, and categories. Each font and font family is presented on a double page. On the left page, each font is applied inspired by this year's theme of film and plants. To the right, the typeface is described in detail; with all its features, as well as information about the designers and foundries. A complementary online microsite features all fonts with direct links to respective foundries and purchasing options.

Slanted Publishers
GERMANY
LANGUAGE SUPPORT XXX
OPENTYPE FEATURES XXX

608 PAGES   slanted.de

9/10 designers already use fonts*

* Damning results from a recent study by the Dinamo Research Institute (DRI).

abcdinamo.com

Arizona	Gaisyr	Pareto
Asphalt	Gravitas	Pelikan
BINGO	Gravity	Prophet
Connect	GROW	Repro
Camera	Helveesti	ROM
Daily Scotch	Honeymoon	Simon
Daily Slab	Ikarus	Social
Diatype	Laica	Solar
Diatype Rounded	Marfa	STEFAN
Display	Marist	Synt
Estragon	Maxi	Walter Alte
Favorit	Monument Grotesk	Walter Neue
Ginto	Meteora	Whyte
Ginto Rounded	Oracle	Whyte Inktrap
Gramercy	Oracle Triple	

Flashy Charismatic Stylish
Elegant
Seductive Chic
Classy
Sophisticated
Soft

Lavigne Nova
Text & Display

Glamo-
Handsome ja
Refined
ashionable Graceful
Captivating
Lovely Sensuous

Retype

› info@re-type.com › Only Available at **re-type.com**

Weil alles auch anders sein kann.

Zukunft gestalten: Master in Design.
Bewerbung bis zum 15.12.2024

www.hs-niederrhein.de/design/ma-design

Konstanze Albrecht und Natalie Josten (MA) entwickelten ein Kommunikationskonzept zur Förderung von interkulturellen Begegnungen im Tourismus.

Master of Arts in Design an der Hochschule Niederrhein.

Communication and Industrial Design
Diploma programs at the Faculty of Design at Darmstadt University of Applied Sciences on UNESCO World Heritage Site Mathildenhöhe
design.h-da.de

Stains in a Row – project by Viktoria Klotz (2nd year student) – see also p. 111

Magazin Studium Bewerbung

GESTALTUNG

Radi-kal und zärtlich zugleich

ICH HABE DAS PARADIES GESEHEN

Zu viel Kaffee trinken, Gedrehte rauchen und *broke* sein

HS'BI

GESTALTUNG-BIELEFELD.DE

Das digitale Magazin für Design, Kunst und Theorie der Hochschule Bielefeld.

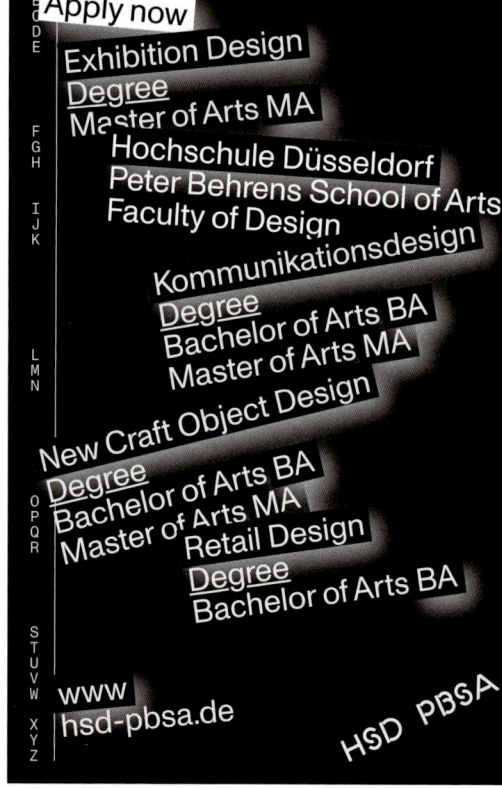

Apply now

Exhibition Design
Degree
Master of Arts MA

Hochschule Düsseldorf
Peter Behrens School of Arts
Faculty of Design

Kommunikationsdesign
Degree
Bachelor of Arts BA
Master of Arts MA

New Craft Object Design
Degree
Bachelor of Arts BA
Master of Arts MA

Retail Design
Degree
Bachelor of Arts BA

www
hsd-pbsa.de

HSD PBSA

graphic design
typography
photography
illustration
visual culture

never not creating

get them all at slanted.de/shop
or support your local dealer

UCON
ACROBATICS

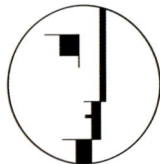

Founded in 1919 by visionary architect Walter Gropius, the Bauhaus art school combined comprehensive craftsmanship with a minimal design approach. The idea was to unify the princi-ples of mass pro-duction with individual artistic vision and to combine aesthetics with every-day function. The elementary core for this cooperation is an in-novative material. The Cork from Portugal is cut into thin layers and then fixed to a silver water-proof film. In the final step, blue paint is applied to the cork sur-face using a rubber roller. The unique structure of cork, with its jagged textures, allows for a unique artistic composition.

The values of Bauhaus – which later became a driving force in modern design, architecture and art – are what Ucon Acrobatics was built on.

www.ucon-acrobatics.com

ESSAYS

THOUGHTS
IDEAS
CONCEPTS
ARTICLES
MUSE

/16/

CHRISTINA DONOGHUE

FASHION'S RELATIONSHIP WITH TYPOGRAPHY: ARMING US FOR THE NEW AGE

CHRISTINA DONOGHUE is an arts editor and journalist from London. She is currently the art and culture editor of SHOWstudio where she oversees the platform's arts coverage. Donoghue has freelanced for numerous publications including Marie Claire and The Times and has also lectured on Central Saint Martins' Fashion Communication course.

After SHOWstudio's surreal-esque makeover last year with a new moving logo, writer Christina Donoghue decided to delve deeper, interviewing Peter Saville, Nick Knight, and Paul Barnes about typography's roots in surrealism and futurism, and how the two have paved the way for modern graphic design in fashion.

Have you ever read a book and found the lettering infuriatingly dense, making it hard to follow? Or one whose typeface is too distracting? Have you ever been browsing several book spines on a shelf and had one jump out at you amid a crowded section? Fonts have different personalities, which is why you never see *Comic Sans* on a funeral notice—or a railway arch graffitied in *Times New Roman.* Some are aggressive, even slightly punkish in character (*Misfit,* we're looking at you). Some are light and breezy *(Calibri).* Others? Well, one can only describe them as goth-like and, quite simply, rather strange. Graphics and typography not only bombard everyday life—they dictate the everyday; that mouldy carton of milk with a half scratched off label sat in your fridge? Someone's designed that. An album's genre-defining cover art? (Yes, we're talking about New Order's *Blue Monday*)—you have the genius that is Peter Saville to thank. Picked up *The Guardian* at the weekend? Typographer Paul Barnes is behind their infamous font—the *Guardian Egyptian* slab-serif typeface, which came along with the paper's distinguished 2005 rebranding also overseen by Barnes. Almost everything and anything man-made you come across has involved at least a basic level of graphic design, and where there's graphics, the conversation of typography follows not too far behind.

"Type is the most profoundly significant aspect of communications design," Saville revealed when I spoke to him last week about the significance of typography in today's world. "It's arguably more important than the hair in a fashion show, and the hair is really important in the fashion show. I don't think there's anything as immediately significant in the reading of a fashion image as the hair, so that says a lot." This comes from the man who once told writer and curator Lou Stoppard in a 2015 SHOWstudio *In Fashion* interview: "Our entire globe is a communications sphere."

Armed with a famed philosophy of wanting to "make fashion move" (and joining Saville a staggering amount of enthusiasm towards our very own communications sphere), is SHOWstudio's founder and director Nick Knight—which is where the context of our new animated logo, designed by Swiss designer Zach Lieberman and filmmaker and motion graphics artist Dirk Koy, comes into play. Determined to break the rules of typography, in 2020, we began asking designers and creative masterminds to reimagine the original SHOWstudio logo, first designed by Saville in 2000.

SHOWstudio has always endeavored to embrace fashion's omnipresent digital future. Fed up with the stagnant images displayed in magazines in the nineties, Knight was fueled with the burning desire to showcase fashion the way he saw it; on set in real-time, live and in motion. The turn of the millennium brought with it dial-up Internet and a future that many people were too scared to accept. Recognizing the advantages of an online world, and, in the words of the late David Bowie, its "enormous potential," SHOWstudio was the first to live stream a fashion shoot *(Sleep)* in 2001; a move so successful it led to Knight collaborating with fashion virtuoso Alexander McQueen. The pair then worked together to make history, resulting in the first ever live-streamed fashion show, *Plato's Atlantis.* In short, SHOWstudio made fashion move, encouraged its movement and delighted in it when the industry started to catch on (albeit after considerable

STILL FROM ZACH LIEBERMAN × SHOWSTUDIO MOVING LOGO ANIMATION

hesitance). Considering this, it felt contradictory to have a logo as inactive as the complacent magazine format that repelled Knight in the first place. So, we asked ourselves, "If fashion can be shown in movement, why can't type?" Queue the moving logo.

Both Lieberman and Koy's work is wildly hypnotic and intensely futuristic, possessing nostalgic surrealist qualities, subsequently straddling many 20th-century art forms as a result. Fundamentally, their moving graphics can be considered a reaction to the technological advancements in computing in the 21st century—similar to all the art movements that have funnily embraced type as part of their own work; Futurism, Constructivism, Dada, and Surrealism all were notably reactions to the old establishment.

As someone who's always been fascinated by the art movements of the early 20th century—wishing to soak up any information that pointed or even alluded to Breton's surrealist manifesto or Marinetti's futurist principles—I found myself likening Knight's intense fascination with the technological advancements of our own time to Marinetti's admiration for machinery and the new industrial age—one that took place a century before SHOWstudio's birth.

In 1909, Filippo Tommaso Marinetti (a leading Italian Futurist) put pen to paper and wrote what soon became the first futurist manifesto, declaring "the end of the past and the beginning of the future," the future being the movement's moniker *(Le Futurisme)*. Written in the manifesto was a hungry desire to neglect all nostalgic forms of art, moving past romanticism by looking to the beauty of the future: "We declare that the splendor of the world has been enriched by a new beauty: the beauty of speed ... a roaring motor car which seems to run on machine-gun fire, is more beautiful than the victory of Samothrace." Wondering if these comparisons were far-fetched or if there was more than meets the eye, I turned to one of the world's most notorious graphic designers to look for answers, Peter Saville.

Some of Saville's most iconic artworks (see Joy Division's Closer, for example) take imagery synonymous with art history, such as the still life, placing them in a modern context by reinterpreting their meaning entirely. These works, emblematic of the period in which Saville was working in, have gone on to inspire a myriad of creatives, notably the Belgian fashion designer Raf Simons. To give even a brief synopsis that encapsulates their rich cultural cache, the records Saville designed while at Factory Records for the likes of Joy

STILL FROM DIRK KOY × SHOWSTUDIO MOVING LOGO ANIMATION

Division and New Order have ended up on cult collector's items; take the A/W 03 Raf Simons parkas. This in itself makes Saville the perfect candidate to speak to when wondering about the influence of graphic design on contemporary culture.

Cementing my thoughts on the synergy between 20th century art, fashion, modern graphic design, and typography, Saville started by telling me that his eureka moment in understanding the importance of art and its relation to everyday graphics happened when he was in the library at Manchester Polytechnic. "When I was in college, somebody told me to go and look in the library and hidden there is what I can now only describe as the canon of graphic design history." Going on to explain this so-called "canon," Saville notes "Its provenance and origins are in early 20th century art movements," and went on to establish that "graphics is a discipline that comes out of the modernist era of art." Making such a statement could imply that Saville believes graphic design didn't exist pre-modernism, yet he knows that's not the case. "Obviously, there was print and posters and newspapers before the early 20th century, but the crucial understanding of graphic design that prevailed through the 20th century has its origins in those very significant art movements." Saville quickly corrects himself, "But really, the art of the early 20th century is more than just movements; they speak of the new industrial order in life."

So, where did Saville's interest in design come from? For people who know the prolific art director and his rich and diverse portfolio of work, it comes as no surprise that Saville didn't stumble upon the art of making record covers out of the blue. In fact, this very exercise led him to be interested in art and graphics in the first place. "I didn't go to art school to learn and study graphic design. At the age of 17, 18, I didn't even know what graphic design was," he admits. Asked when he started to see graphics as a "job," he tells me about his introduction to 1970s record cover art. "Like any other teenager, particularly in the 70s, we were obsessed with record covers, the reason being that they were pretty much," he pauses, "well actually, not pretty much, they were singularly the only medium of progressive visual imagery that permeated our lives. We liked visual culture, and the only place where we saw progressive visual culture was on a record sleeve—we saw them as a medium in their own right."

Explaining the cultural significance of not only a record but the artwork it came with, Saville notes that he and his friend spoke of them "as if they were independent things ... So we may have been indifferent to the music, but we would first and foremost always speak about the cover. It wasn't just covers of records of the bands we liked; we identified the covers themselves as art that we did or didn't like, and over time, it became apparent that that was what we were into. We would spend all of our spare time in the art room at school and lunchtimes and stay for an hour after school and things like that, doing illustrations and paintings for fantasy record covers." Little did he know that the following decade would see him create some of the world's most influential cover art that's ever been designed.

Inspired by Saville's work from the eighties, leading typographer Paul Barnes also started to make his own record covers when at school. "I didn't study art at school, but I

STILL FROM DIRK KOY × SHOWSTUDIO MOVING LOGO ANIMATION

always had an interest in letters, which I saw as a way into graphic design. With things like what Saville did, a lot of it was purely typographical—which inspired me and my own path. Eventually, one of the art tutors came up to me to try and convince me to apply to the typography course at Reading University, and I already had a portfolio because I started making things like imaginary record covers and different things."

When Barnes went on to study typography seriously, he realized that "Not everything was about making record covers all the time, you did quite dry things also, like learning about how to specify the type for a book and other formats." Though typography does not always allude to fantasy record covers (at least not in Barnes's case), type is still a definitive factor. Highlighting the specific power the choice of type holds over many designers when they're faced with the task of making new work, Saville reminisces on his younger years and how the discovery of a book that held what he refers to as "the secrets to typography," old and new, immediately resonated with him as a new graphic designer that was only starting out. "When I was at the beginning of my career, I stumbled across this enormous encyclopedia of typography. We're talking about hundreds of years worth of development in type. I could also see how they all—these profoundly evident and sometimes subtly different semiotic qualities—informed any piece of graphic work that I wished to do. Everything I've done; it's always the choice in the typeface first." The collaborative performance between word and image is also a heady one. An interplay that feeds into the very nature of graphic design and the importance of curating a page, it's imperative to reference the dutiful relationship between words and images and how the two (if done successfully) should work with each other, rather than against one another. Words, when given thought, also act as a form of imagery. Composition, typeface, and overall layout are integral to the idea of seeing type as an expressive form of design. No one knew this better than the artistic genius Alexey Brodovitch, most notably when he held the appointed position of art director at *Harper's Bazaar* from 1934–1958.

In 1934, the newly appointed editor of *Harper's Bazaar,* Carmel Snow, attended an exhibition curated by Brodovitch for The Art Directors Club of New York. Snow described it as a revelation, writing, "Pages that bled beautifully, cropped photographs, typography, and design that were bold and arresting." Before he knew it, Brodovitch would become art director of the famed magazine, where he gave a platform to many of the surrealists,

STILL FROM DIRK KOY × SHOWSTUDIO MOVING LOGO ANIMATION

situating them in a fashion context while transforming the magazine altogether. Creating double-page spreads that bore witness to words wrapped slinkily around the silhouette of an image, Brodovitch revolutionized the importance and imposing elegance of the written word, something that's seemingly been lost over the years. From someone whose work has featured in countless magazines over the last four decades, Knight told me, "The curation of a page can either make or massacre my work—once I've handed my work over, it's no longer up to me, it becomes someone else's job."

When understanding the surrealist aspect of both Lieberman and Koy's works, it's important to note that although both artists choosing to couple their practice with CGI is new, their fascination with using words to create modern poetry isn't. The term "modern poetry" has floated about before, bouncing between many of the earlier 20th-century art movements Saville talks about. Famed for his avant-garde approach towards creating "typographical poetry," Guillaume Apollinaire—who made enormous contributions to the French literary and artistic circles at the beginning of the 20th century—designed *Il Pleut*, a barely legible poem with cascades of letters—emphasized to evoke the feeling of rain. *Il Pleut* is a shaped poem, where the order, look, and style are as integral to the form as the actual writing (or tumbling words), referring to these poems as *Calligrames*.

Typography has always stood at the forefront of change, and futurism was no exception for embracing new ways of thinking and communication in line with a "typographical revolution." When asking Saville about typography's role in supporting graphics and significant art movements, he told me "there's a remarkable and noteworthy synergy within fashion, culture, and typography, and it's to a great extent," adding, "the application of type is the styling of communications design through and through." Marinetti understood this, pushing his love for the written word and typography beyond "freeing the verse" and rejecting all the traditionalist values that had come before, he wrote in the Futurist manifesto: "I call for a typographic revolution directed against the idiotic and nauseating concepts of the outdated and conventional book, with its handmade paper and seventeenth ornamentation of garlands and goddesses, huge initials and mythological vegetation, its missal ribbons and epigraphs and roman numerals. The book must be the futurist expression of our futurist ideas."

Constructivist in style, futurism was easily recognizable through its abrasive appearance. Think Jackson Pollock furiously attacking his canvas. Think hard and think fast. Think speed, destruction, machinery, violence, and industrialization. Think of the mechanical age and the industrial revolution. Although visually, the differences are stark, and our current optimism in the future doesn't rely on maximalist approaches, rather minimalist ones, the obsession with the future and technological advancements could be likened to now. If anything, it is the now. We live in a growing culture of NFT's, AI, and CGI, resulting in a fashion industry that's more in touch with the future than with the past. Impactful and meaningful fashion has never looked to the past but rather, the future. Saville also touches upon this, although his reasoning for it is one I never thought of before, yet once realized, one knows it couldn't be any other way.

"Since the post-modern reset of a pluralist culture, postmodernism positioned itself as the end of 'post-isms.' Since postmodernism, there has not been one singular, overwhelming ideology that has controlled the way we do things. Modernism was one of those, and along with the others, it said, 'you can only build this way, everybody has to wear these clothes and travel in these cars on these roads.' After modernism, society said, 'fuck it, we've had enough of this notion, this ideological notion that said there's one size fits all,' by the time you get to the seventies, it's like, no, I'm sorry, this is not like that and postmodernism is that watershed moment."

To try and live in the present can be daunting at best. The future? Terrifying and electrifying in equal parts. After two decades, the Internet has reached the brink of a second revolution. At the beginning of the last century, the Western world was on the brink of something too—although unknown what quite that was—the industrial revolution had only taken place some decades before; futurism as a movement signaled all of this. It was a new technological age. Fast forward 110 years to the present day, and the same thing is occurring. Which leads me to ask, is this our futurism? The 21st-century futurism that, instead of looking to cars and machinery, looks to the future of the Internet? When the Internet came about towards the end of the 90s, people feared it and yet, it's become so ingrained into our lives that Labour even campaigned for the "digital bill of rights" in their 2016 manifesto, with Corbyn pledging to "democratize the Internet" if he came into power. At one point, the Internet was the future; now, it's the present. Who knows, maybe one day it'll be the past. Typography has played a part in the fundamentals of graphic design since the beginning of the 20th century, helping us transfer from one "ism" to the next. We can't predict what's around the corner but we know typographical developments played a significant role in our culture's past, and who's to say typography won't arm us for the future too.

The article was originally published online by Christina Donoghue on showstudio.com on August 10th, 2021.

ANN MARIE WAINSCOTT

VICTORIA'S OTHER SECRET: HER TYPEFACE

DR. ANN MARIE WAINSCOTT is the Karen and Adeed Dawisha Associate Professor of Political Science at Miami University. This article builds on her book project *The Titan of Test City: Leslie Wexner and the Making of Columbus.* Her first book Bureaucratizing Islam: Morocco and the War on Terror was published in 2017 by Cambridge University Press.

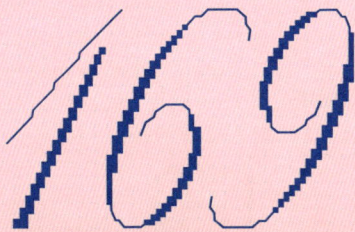

F

For decades, the American lingerie company Victoria's Secret was synonymous with the Angels, the supermodels that represented the brand in its annual fashion show and modeled its apparel in catalogs and commercials. But with a dramatic (failed) rebrand in recent years, a pause in the iconic fashion show, the elimination of catalogs, and a move away from the Angels as brand ambassadors, the most enduring aspect of the brand may well be its custom typeface, *Victoria One*, first introduced in 2011, but referencing similar fonts that the brand began using in the late 1980s.

The enduring nature of Victoria One speaks to the genius of Leslie Wexner, former CEO of Limited Brands, a company that at its height included a vast portfolio of retail powerhouses from the Limited, to Bed, Bath & Beyond, to Abercrombie & Fitch. Wexner specialized in acquiring little known brands and making them into household names. He explained, "All our acquisitions, except Mast [Industries], were failures when we acquired them … [We] purposely picked businesses that were losers but that we thought we could turn around, because there was more value in them—that is, we could get paid for our work rather than paying somebody else for theirs. I don't think there has ever been a retail business that has as consistent a record of picking niches of retailing and either remerchandizing [them] or starting a business to hit niches the way we've done it. I'm very proud of that fact."

Victoria's Secret followed this familiar pattern. Wexner acquired the business for a million dollars in the early 1980's and transformed it from a few stores and a catalog into the most successful intimate apparel brand of a generation.

The *Victoria One* typeface is so ubiquitous that it is hard to imagine the company without it, but there was a time before it graced company catalogs, before Wexner acquired the company. Victoria's Secret was founded by Roy Raymond in 1977, after he noticed how uncomfortable he was buying lingerie for his wife in department stores. While maintaining a few storefronts in the San Francisco Bay area, the majority of the business was done through catalog sales (and, as Les Wexner later made public, a sex toy business). The catalog was sensuous, but seen as classy compared to competitors. Advertising guru Joseph Sugarman called the company "an upscale version of a Frederick's of Hollywood lingerie catalog." But the company had a narrow vision of sexy; the models were always blond and white.

Wexner had been interested in expanding his business to intimate apparel but it wasn't until he encountered Victoria's Secret that he made moves into the industry. He hoped to create an American version of the European label La Perla that made lingerie accessible and affordable. He described his first experience of the store in these terms: "We had [Limited] stores in San Francisco, and that's where I found an interesting little lingerie store called Victoria's Secret. It was a small store, and it was Victorian--not English Victorian but brothel Victorian, with red-velvet sofas. There wasn't erotic lingerie, but there was very sexy lingerie, and I hadn't seen anything like it in all my travels." Victorian style, named for Queen Victoria who reigned over England for the majority of the nineteenth century, was opulent, reflecting the economic prosperity that elites experienced amidst industrialization. The deep colors and heavy fabrics of Victoria's Secret interiors were appropriate to the Victorian aesthetic. Wexner hadn't seen anything like it because there were very few places to buy lingerie, especially in the United States, outside of traditional department stores in the early 1980s. It was this need that Victoria's Secret would ultimately address.

In line with the company's Victorian vibes, the company's logo at that time was a gilded and embellished script intended to evoke the Victorian ethos, but it tried too hard, coming off as excessive instead of elegant. The fonts of the company's catalogs and ads show little concern for typography. In the catalog, the company used a narrow, italic, sans serif font called *Gestype*. In ads, the font appears to be the italic *Times New Roman*. This inconsistency reflected the generally unprofessional branding that characterized the Roy Raymond era.

WEXNER'S LADIES' PARADISE

In the initial years after L Brands acquired Victoria's Secret, the original logo was kept, but the font in the catalog was immediately changed to a serif font that foreshadowed the company's eventual branding. The new owners experimented temporarily with a tabloid-esque font for the company's name—bold, tall, and narrow—but by the late 1980s had already settled on the now classic all caps design.

The typeface was in line with a new vision for Victoria's Secret. Wexner's vision was inspired by Emile Zola's 1882 serial *Au Bonheur des Dames (The Ladies' Paradise)*. He explained, "If men like Victoria's Secret, that's kind of a bonus. But in my imagination, they should feel uncomfortable when they're in the store … There's nothing that's welcoming; this is a ladies' paradise. And that thinking goes into the design of the store, the fitting room, the fabrics, the display, it's all from the ladies' point of view." Given the number of male executives at the company, what was actually implemented was something more like what men perceive to be a ladies' paradise, but this was still a clear change from Raymond's vision that centered the male consumer.

Victoria's Secret went on to expand at an astronomical rate. While the company's branding certainly contributed to its success, Wexner also implemented many of the strategies at Victoria's Secret that had propelled his first company, the Limited, to success. He pioneered having stores in multiple cities. Roy Raymond's model of having a few stores in one metropolitan area was the norm for retailers in the 1960s and 1970s, but Wexner had already realized that he could dramatically increase revenue through copying successful models of stores and placing them in cities with similar demographics. Struggling stores could then be carried by more successful stores, and the company could expand its customer base. Wexner also kept the inventory to a relatively select and profitable selection (hence the name of his original store, the Limited) and he added fresh merchandise constantly. In order to find new ideas, Wexner and his team traveled to Europe regularly. The company's approach was described in the *New York Times* by journalist Stephanie Strom: "Based in Columbus, Ohio, the Limited is infamous on Seventh Avenue [in New York City] for knocking off designer fashions, making cheap copies in overseas factories and selling them here under its own labels for a fraction of the price." Journalist Robert Lenzner was even more succinct; he commented, "Les is the greatest rip-off artist in the world." These skills served him well at Victoria's Secret, where he followed a similar model of recreating designer fashions at affordable prices.

VICTORIA ONE

Though likely inspired by high-end designer brands, Wexner did not rip off the company's typeface. The company commissioned Neil Summerour of Positype Foundry to develop the *Victoria One* typeface in 2011. The typeface built on an incomplete font that had been based on *Trajan* developed by Font Bureau in 2010. Summerour's typeface was influenced by work that Mucca Design had done on the brand's master wordmark and VS monogram several years earlier. Summerour's typeface included an entirely new lowercase that, when used in Italics, as it often appears, resembles the work of a calligrapher, and a full character set including a distinctive ampersand and dollar sign. The typeface is elegant and classic.

While it is hard to imagine Victoria's Secret without *Victoria One,* the collaboration almost never happened. Summerour was a relatively unknown typographer when he was approached by the company and he ignored their initial emails not realizing they were an actual inquiry. Once they managed to get a hold of him, the partnership developed quickly. They first hired him to complete hand lettering. Then they requested a script typeface for their catalogs. The typeface that he developed is now licensed by Positype as *Flirt.* In yet another project, they wanted a font written in red lipstick (he used Revlon Lustrous 740), a feat which turned out to be so complicated that it built trust with the creative team he was working with there. He went on to design two custom typefaces used by both Victoria's Secret and Pink, *Victoria One* and *VS Lust,* an over-the-top, curvy typeface that built on the work Summerour had already begun on his *Lust* series, which was released publicly in 2015. Victoria's Secret was particularly interested in the scalloped lacrimal, the teardrop on the tip of the lowercase "a" and "c," that contributes to the over-the-top feel of the font. While they didn't request more custom fonts, they later licensed *Lust Slim.*

Summerour's long fascination with the human body served him well during the collaboration, though he is quick to clarify that he does not embrace the way in which his work might be gendered by its association with the company. He explained, "I do love finding inspiration from natural forms. The body is no exception. There's a sensual fluidity that cannot be reproduced but from the human body … I do not care if you want to associate that with a man or woman. It's there and I have a tendency to tap into it. My work with VS, at the time, made total sense and the creative partnership flourished for a time."

CRISIS: FROM LADIES' PARADISE TO FEMALE EMPOWERMENT

Summerour's concern with the company's approach to gender foreshadowed coming difficulties. In 2021, Victoria's Secret split from L Brands, trading as an independent company, VSCO on the New York Stock Exchange. Since that time, the price of the brand has fluctuated wildly, from a high of $ 74.77 per share in the initial days of the offer in August of 2021 to a low of $ 14.58 in October of 2023. The separation came after Leslie Wexner and his wife Abigail both declined to stand for reelection to the board of L Brands, Inc., the former parent company of Victoria's Secret. Wexner had previously stepped down as CEO of L Brands in May of 2020 amidst concerns about his ties to convicted pedophile Jeffrey Epstein, who reportedly posed as a recruiter for Victoria's Secret to lure his victims, though he had no formal connection to the company. That year (2021) also included a *New York Times* investigation detailing what it called a "culture of misogyny" at the company. The move thus marked the end of Wexner's influence at Victoria's Secret and L Brands more broadly at a moment of crisis for both entities.

Given the circumstances, it wasn't surprising when Victoria's Secret didn't just separate from L Brands, it also initiated an extensive rebranding effort, attempting to position itself as a champion of female empowerment. In place of the Angels, the company embraced new brand ambassadors, the VS Collective, that included women of varying body types and forms of power. Stores that were once full of images of impossibly thin mostly white women now feature women of different ethnicities and body types, and the company began to offer nursing bras and depicting pregnant women in its advertising for the first time, moves that were unthinkable under Wexner and the narrow view of sexy that was embraced by the company under his leadership. But despite the rebrand, the company continued to lose market share to competitors.

There were a range of reasons for Victoria's Secret's decline beyond the rebrand. Les Wexner had been, as *The New York Times* once called him, "the Merlin of the Mall," but the mall was already being replaced by online shopping prior to the pandemic, which dealt the institution its final blow in all but the most lucrative markets. The growth of social media eliminated the need for the Victoria's Secret catalog, and the fashion show was eliminated amidst concerns of being out of touch with a more body positive generation of consumers who desired to see a range of bodies in advertising. It didn't help that in 2018, Ed Razek, the company's chief marketing officer, made explicit what everyone already knew—that the company would not feature trans or plus-sized models in its signature fashion show. The gap between young consumers and the brand was widening.

The Victoria's Secret's rebrand has now been labeled a failure. The changes alienated its customer base, many of whom did not agree with the need to eliminate the Angels or to embrace more inclusivity. Now the brand is attempting a delicate balancing act, reintroducing the fashion show in the fall of 2024, including with Angels, but also including a wider range of body types, attempting to balance the competing demands of a diverse customer base.

Amidst these changes, *Victoria One* continues to be the dominant typeface in the company's marketing. Recent reporting on Victoria's Secret emphasizes the brand's fall from grace and failed rebrand. Even with these challenges, the company has one of the world's most enduring brands, a brand that is built in part on its distinctive custom typeface, *Victoria One*. There can be no doubt that it is one of the most successful unions of a mass fashion brand and a typeface in modern history. *Victoria One* illustrates how a brand can become synonymous with a typeface, and when cultural mores call for changes to brand ambassadors, models, and other elements, a well-chosen typeface endures.

GRAPHÉINE.COM

BARBARA KRUGER / SUPREME: WHO'S HIJACKING WHOM?

GRAPHÉINE is a branding agency established in 2002 by a collective of like-minded and energetic designers from various professional backgrounds, all with a shared passion for imagery. Based in Paris and Lyon, France, the team members bring together their diverse skills to create a unified and dynamic whole. Their blog provides a daily infusion of insights into branding and visual identity.

The influence of Barbara Kruger's work in the world of graphic art is such that you've already come across either one of her works or a work or identity inspired by it; starting with the logo of the brand Supreme. But in the game of appropriation, the winner is not always the one you think.

SHARPEN YOUR EYES

Barbara Kruger studied for two years at Parson's School of Design in New York and began working as a graphic designer for *Mademoiselle* magazine, where she became the art director after just one year and held the position for six years. She then went on to design for *Aperture and House & Garden* magazines. Barbara Kruger learned to manipulate images to attract attention through framing and typographical play. She became a visual artist in 1970, but her first handmade productions did not satisfy her.
Barbara Kruger stopped teaching for a few years, then started taking photographs. In 1978 she published a book, *Picture/Readings,* in which her photos echo her texts, like snippets of conversations, moments of life. This publication set the tone for the works that followed, in which the text dialogs with the image, and which launched her reputation.

DEVELOPING HER ICONIC STYLE IN RED, BLACK, AND WHITE

With her experience as a graphic designer and her photographer's eye, she created her famous graphic style in 1979: capital letters in *Futura Bold* or *Helvetica Ultra Condensed* on a background of 1950s advertising images, which she enlarges on large banners, using three colors: black, red, and white. Her first exhibition took place the same year at the P.S.1 Contemporary Art Center at MoMA (New York). On her photomontages she slips large messages that give food for thought: my face is your fortune, your role is to divide and conquer, free love, you kill time. Barbara Kruger's work is engaged, political, philosophical, and sends us back to our consumerist and sexist habits, in a world that is just as much. She allows us to take distance by questioning (among other things) gender, the relationship to power and sex, racism, and our relationship to objects, through images and texts put in resonance. If the association image-text-incitation reminds us of advertising slogans, it allows here to make passers-by think.
The use of the pronoun "I" or "you" makes it possible to include the spectator (and especially the spectatrix!) in his works, and to invite him to question himself on his habits or his situation. Barbara Kruger will say ironically in an interview of 1991 that she is "interested in images and words because they have the specific power to define who we are and who we are not," and that she developed "the power to handle words," because it is "what girls do, failing to be able to handle weapons. She takes up Goethe's sentence, "we are slaves to the objects that surround us" or declines Marilyn's face in the manner of Warhol, by silk-screening impactful words, by contrast.

DENOUNCING THE CONSUMER SOCIETY

Like Warhol, Kruger's art, reproducible en masse via silkscreen or digital printing, questions the essence of art and intellectual property. Kruger does not own the rights to the Futura typography or the artistic principle of placing colored text-rectangles on photos, reminiscent of constructivist collages. Her work deliberately blurs the lines between artist, viewer, and artwork, no longer confined to galleries but presented as a consumer good or even an advertisement, engaging in a dialog with the consumer-collector.

In 1987 Barbara Kruger created one of her most famous works, which remains relevant today: *Untitled (I shop therefore I am)*. The 1980s was the decade of consumer credit and new markets, and consumers gained more power. On this work, a genderless hand holds a card, like a business card, which mentions: I shop therefore I am, diverting the famous thought of Descartes, "I think therefore I am." She will also print this image on kraft bags for shopping.

By replacing thought with consumption, Barbara Kruger critiques the loss of meaning in a consumer society that values having over being. She deplores the fact that the human being becomes a robot who no longer thinks but buys to exist. In the same way, she underlines that advertising generates doubts and guilt towards the representation of oneself in an ideal and unattainable world. The frenetic consumption comes to fill this gap between the expectation and the reality, and can contribute to deform this image of oneself.

The red text on a white background acts as a manifesto, using marketing strategies. Barbara Kruger first creates a visual contrast between black and white and color, which allows a double reading in two times between the image and the text. The color red, color of danger and desire, stimulates the reptilian brain and irresistibly attracts the eye. The red letters are reminiscent of advertising ads that abuse these techniques to better attract the eye of the consumer and make their message stand out in this visual ocean.

FIGHTING FOR WOMEN'S RIGHTS

Two years later, in support of a free-choice abortion march in Washington in 1989, she created her second most influential work: *Untitled (your body is a battleground)*, as anti-abortion waves swept through the United States. It will be declined in French (savoir c'est pouvoir), and even in Polish, to defend the same causes. This silk-screened poster features a female face separated into two equal parts and treated in negative. Taken from an advertising poster, probably a cosmetics ad, this face first denounces the use of the woman's body as a stereotyped product of society, and dictated by its laws. The woman does not belong to herself anymore. The face cut in two perfectly symmetrical parts illustrates the opposite injunctions that are placed on her face (and more broadly her body), according to the parties. Originally, pro-abortion and anti-abortion. The play of negative colors distorts her face, half angel, half demon, and raises the ambivalences of the posture of the woman, sometimes docile, sometimes fighting.

By taking a step back, we can read more widely the oppositions between women and men, women and the stereotyped view of men on women, the masculinist society that transforms women into objects and women into flesh. The phase "your body is a battlefield" comes to underline the fights which take place on this body, her body, which she must reappropriate above all. Barbara Kruger thus denounces the position and the fights of the woman in a world which considers her only by her appearance. More broadly, she raises the question of the norm and the look that society gives to all those who emancipate themselves from it. A statement across Andy Warhol's face: "not beautiful enough—not pathetic enough—not man enough—not real enough—not cruel enough." And over Marilyn Monroe's: "not good enough—not skinny enough—not anything at all—not ironic enough—not stupid enough." A pair of glasses, inscripted with: "your look hits my profile," which invites the male gaze, the famous "male gaze" to question itself.

SUPREME AND BARBARA KRUGER: SAME STYLE, DIFFERENT FIGHT!

If reading this article makes you think that this style reminds you of something, you're absolutely right: the Supreme brand. Or maybe you've recently read our analysis of the adopte un mec's logo, also directly inspired by the latter? In 1994 the founder of Supreme (James Jebbia) was looking for a new logo for his store and his skate and streetwear brand. A brand of men, for men. He lends a book on the work of Barbara Kruger to his graphic designer and the logo is born as if by magic. The Supreme logo is written in white letters, bold and oblique *Futura* on a red background: Same letters, but not the same fight. Kruger does not flinch, magnanimous. She doesn't own the rights, and doesn't want to get down to launching legal and financial battles. Especially since it is common among streetwear brands to reappropriate the codes of other brands. In 2000, Supreme tried to take over Louis Vuitton's designs, before being called to order.

22 years later, world-famous brands such as Louis Vuitton, Gucci, Coca-Cola or even the artists Pollock, John Baldessari, Robert Longo, and Damian Hirst collaborate hand in hand with Supreme by returning the levers of glory, and without rancor! A skateboard decorated by Damien Hirst bought for $700 and sold for $20,000 a few years later. Barbara Kruger knew how to use art to take sides and denounce injustice, unlike the Supreme brand which uses graphics and art for purely commercial purposes.

Where the artist Kruger criticized capitalism, consumerism, and ambient machismo, Supreme (the coolest brand—according to the generation Y) bathes happily in it. Intended for men, the rare communication campaigns representing women are used to "censor" their private parts with the brand's banner, thus inviting the male gaze to rest on this female body, once again a battlefield and a lever for sexist consumption.

There is no second degree in Supreme: the woman is clearly prostituted in commercial object. As we said in our article on adopte un mec, "a committed and popular approach often leads to its opposite, Supreme, by imitating Barbara Kruger, operates a technique well known in the world of capitalism (and advertising in general): the recovery. Brands appropriate a discourse from a minority—feminism, anti-consumerism—and inject it into their majority and macho system, which contributes to neutralize it, to phagocytize it, in order to better promote the initial system against which they were fighting."

WHO IS COPYING WHO?

The famous image of Kate Moss on a Supreme shirt is itself taken from a Calvin Klein advertisement that Supreme appropriated … To push the envelope a little further, in 2004 the brand Married to the Mob also plays the game of graphic appropriation and launches T-shirts and caps named "Supreme Bitch." The designer got the authorization from his friend Jebbia (founder of Supreme). Rihanna, Cara, and a whole bunch of international stars are rushing to wear them. Who's whose bitch? Ironically ironic.

But in 2013 Supreme flips and sues them with a $10 million lawsuit for "counterfeiting, unfair competition and forgery of a designation of origin, logo dilution, and trademark infringement!" What's amazing is that the Supreme trademark was only registered in 2011 and the logo … in 2013 at the conclusion of this lawsuit. We feel the bad players afraid to lose at their own game! Barbara Kruger reacts this time by deploring a "ridiculous amalgam of small not cool buffoons" who wallow in stories of rights and money. She claims to be "waiting for everyone to come and sue her for copyright infringement." Married to the Mob claimed to have launched "Supreme Bitch" to "criticize and parody the male dominance and misogyny of skate culture guys and the Supreme brand …"

WHO IS SMARTER THAN WHO?

In 2017, as part of an Art Biennial, Barbara Kruger launched an installation in a boutique gallery and skate park in New York City, displaying slogans like "who's copying who?"—"who belongs to whom?"—"money talks"—"bully"—"whose values?"—"who's above the law?" and "don't be a jerk," featured on banners, T-shirts (from the brand Volcom), and skateboards. People paid $5 to stand in line in front of what looked like a Supreme store, unaware they were ironically caught in the consumer trap.

Who is smarter than who? We have our own idea. I guess appropriation has its limits and consequences! Moral: don't be a jerk!

The article was originally published online on grapheine.com on January 19th, 2022.

JELENA DROBAC

NOWHERE & EVERYWHERE: UNVEILING FASHION LOGOS OF SFR YUGOSLAVIA

JELENA DROBAC is a Serbian graphic designer and educator with 20 years of experience in identity, typography, and packaging. A professor and Head of the Design Department at the Academy Polytechnic Belgrade, she holds degrees in Graphic design (MA) and Interdisciplinary arts (DA) from the University of Arts in Belgrade. Her work has been featured in over 50 publications and has won more than 20 awards internationally.

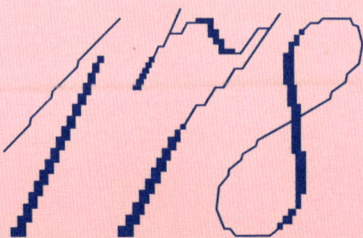

For starters, what was the Socialist Federal Republic of Yugoslavia? Geography defines it as a country in the Balkan Peninsula, spanning 255,804 square kilometers from the Alps in the northwest, along the Adriatic coast, through the last European rainforest, across northern sunflower and crop plains, to a picturesque convergence of lakes, sea, and mountains in the south. The state emerged in 1945, succeeding the Kingdom of Yugoslavia, and existed until 1992 when it was broken into six parts, its former six republics: Bosnia and Herzegovina, Croatia, Macedonia, Montenegro, Serbia, and Slovenia. During its existence, the motto of the country was "Brotherhood and Unity" but eventually being dismembered in a bloody civil war. Named "the Land of the Southern Slavs", it had a population of about 24 million, sharing similar DNA, language, and heritage, yet divided by religion and historical allegiances. Yugoslav culture was diverse, bearing similarities from the same or similar identity, ethnicity and language, two alphabets in use (Latin and Cyrillic), but differences as a result of interferences of foreign religious, political and cultural identities (Turkish, Austro-Hungarian, Russian etc).

Historically, Socialist Yugoslavia was initially centralized politically and economically, under Tito's Communist Party, with a constitution akin to the Soviet Union's. This led to the nationalization of private ownership and land. The post-war country was rebuilt through voluntary labor, with free housing, healthcare and education aiming for equal distribution. Despite its Soviet-style beginning, Yugoslavia soon distanced itself from the Soviet Union following the Tito-Stalin split. During the Cold War, Yugoslavia chose a neutral path, founding the Non-Aligned Movement, a group of 120 countries in an attempt to follow their path, independent of major powers. This facilitated a unique economic model blending market mechanisms with state planning and worker self-management. As a result, Yugoslavia was one of Europe's fastest-growing countries in the 1950s and 1960s, producing its goods (from cars to appliances, from food and electricity to fashion) and allowing unrestricted access to Western content. Yugoslavs enjoyed the freedom to travel globally without limitations.

Opinions on Yugoslavia vary among its former citizens. *Yugonostalgics,* as some call them, remember it as a land of freedom, opportunities, stability, care for its citizens, broad social giving and beauty. Some recall it as a place of political, religious, and national repression. The Socialist Federal Republic of Yugoslavia dissolved when Croatia and Slovenia declared independence in 1991, followed by Croatia's civil war. In 1992, Bosnia and Herzegovina proclaimed independence, leading to a three-year war among its ethnic and religious groups.

Since the wars ended, there has never been more talk about Yugoslavia in the media, especially in the USA like today. The hype surrounding Yugoslavia has been slowly brewing since New York's MoMA exhibition *Toward a Concrete Utopia: Architecture in Yugoslavia 1948–1980* in 2018. This massive project, curated by Vladimir Kulić and Martino Stierli with assistant Anna Kats was an examination of the brutalist, socialist architecture of the former Yugoslavia with more than 400 drawings, models, photographs, and video installations. The focus was the three-decade span of architecture that "conjures a vision of Balkan utopianism where the aura of concrete takes on almost mythic qualities"[1] to quote a review by Canadian Architect Associate Editor Stefan Novakovic.

This exhibition created waves and shifted perspectives on Yugoslavia as a country and way of living and thinking, not only among fellow architects but also among the general public. The echo reached new generations of young people living in the area that once

SELECTION OF YUGOSLAVIAN LOGOS

was called Yugoslavia but born after its demise. Many of them took part or became passionate followers of the Spomenik Database—an online platform dedicated to the exploration of Yugoslavia's abstract anti-fascist WWII monuments dating from 1960 to 1990. Recently, two unlikely underdogs—neither stereotypical athletic types—have taken over the NBA and revolutionized basketball in the USA by embracing a distinctly Yugoslavian approach. They focus on self-reliance, playing smarter rather than harder, and imposing their unique style on the game. Nikola Jokić from Serbia, a three-time NBA MVP, and Luka Dončić from Slovenia, besides being the top two players in the NBA today, are best friends and superstars. They enjoy listening to regional music during breaks, socializing, and engaging in typical local jokes and pastimes. They are leading a wave of players from the former Yugoslavia in the NBA, including Dragić, Bogdanović, Jović, Micić, Nurkić, Vučević, etc. Recently, Goran Dragić even gave a brief lecture on Yugoslavian history during a basketball TV show in the US. When Jokić's team, the Denver Nuggets, lost in the semifinals, Dončić publicly announced that he "will avenge his fallen Yugoslav brother." Interestingly, both Jokić and Dončić were born after the dissolution of Yugoslavia. Building on that theme and representing the younger generation, Ognjen Ranković, a designer from Belgrade born in the 1990s, also paid homage to Yugoslavian heritage in a public manner. His project, YugoLogo,[2] initially began as a means to preserve logos of defunct companies that he photographed on old modernist buildings throughout the region. "These logos are part of our collective consciousness and symbolize the industrial and cultural heritage of an era. I felt it was a great loss that these symbols, along with their creators, were fading into obscurity," Ognjen explained.

His concept gained more substance when he encountered the book *Graphic Identification 1961-1981* by professor, designer, and design chronicler Miloš Ćirić. Ognjen commenced uploading digitized logos on Instagram. Fast forward, and 460 logos later, it evolved into a self-published book that sold its first edition of 500 copies in less than two months. By ex-Yugoslav standards, this was an exceptionally rapid and successful endeavor. The YugoLogo exhibition is presently touring former Yugoslavia. To date, it has been showcased in Zagreb and Pula (Croatia), Skopje and Bitola (North Macedonia), and Bihać in Bosnia and Herzegovina. Exhibitions are also planned for Banja Luka and Sarajevo

(Bosnia and Herzegovina) and Rijeka (Croatia) later this year. The fact that most of these symbols, designed over half a century ago, yet still withstand the test of time, serves as a central motivation behind the entire project.

Ranković acknowledges that the feedback received across the former country exceeds expectations and provides a significant morale boost. The growing general interest in the project spans a diverse audience, ranging from individuals who lived through that era to design professionals, from the general public to foreigners unfamiliar with Yugoslavia. Ognjen believes that the post-Yugoslavian generation possesses the discernment to recognize quality in various domains, including architecture, fashion, and design, and that Yugoslavia was in tune with the world and its zeitgeist.

The popularity of this project demonstrates that good logo design is timeless. YugoLogo tapped into the hipster subculture both globally and regionally. Numerous online stores have emerged, selling retro Yugoslav everyday objects, designer items, and clothing. Vintage and mid-century apparel have been highly valued and priced for years, not only for their aesthetic appeal but also because of the high-quality garments and materials from that era.

RISE OF FASHION

Considering that SFR Yugoslavia engaged in various fields, oscillating from in-between to ever-present—from military prowess to soft power, from scientific endeavors to sports, and from artistic expression to architectural and engineering feats. Wherever there was an opportunity to enter the global stage, demonstrate competence, and compete, Yugoslavia seized it, and the realm of fashion was no exception.

In the initial years of SFRY, efforts were focused on rebuilding infrastructure, rapid industrialization, establishment of factories, and training of the predominantly female workforce. Until 1960, the fashion sector primarily comprised of textile and clothing industry, with leather and fabrics being the main products manufactured and exported.

As the middle class gained strength and the influence of Soviet socialism waned, Yugoslavs began embracing Western fashion aesthetics, recognizing their ability to actively participate in the global fashion arena rather than merely importing trends. The government utilized fashion not solely as an industry but also as a tool of soft power, asserting Yugoslavia's position in the Cold War world and advocating for a third option.

Yugoslavia participated in Eastern Block shows and fairs, ventured into Western markets, fashion events, and extended its reach to Africa and Asia. The burgeoning popularity of the fashion industry in Yugoslavia was significantly propelled by the 1960 film *Ljubavi-moda* (eng.: "Love & Fashion"). This musical comedy, set in Belgrade, depicted a group of students striving to organize a fashion show for the fictitious company YugoChic. In a socialist manner, it romanticized the fashion industry and popularized Western lifestyles and dressing, particularly the Italian style. The film attained iconic status for its soundtrack and aesthetics, leading to its official recognition as "a Cultural Asset of Great Importance" in Serbia in 2016.

Just to illustrate the Yugoslavian fashion industry size, at the Moscow Fashion Festival 1970, Yugoslavia had 300 fashion houses as exhibitors while in 1985, the fashion sector had about 1 million employees. Most of these did not survive the turbulent 1990s.

DESIGNERS IN SOCIALISM

In former Yugoslavia, the role of the designer as an author was shaped by the unique socio-political environment, which emphasized collective effort over individual recognition. Designers in socialist Yugoslavia often viewed their work as part of a collective endeavor. The socialist ideology promoted the idea that the output of design and industry was a collective property, contributing to the community and the state's goals. Many designers worked without seeking personal recognition, reflecting the socialist emphasis on

SELECTION OF YUGOSLAVIAN LOGOS

collective achievement. Design works were often owned by state enterprises, which further diluted individual credit.

Despite the collectivist approach, Yugoslav designers were significantly influenced by modernist principles and international design trends, particularly from the 1960s onwards. This influence introduced a degree of individual expression within the framework of collective ideology. Their specific aspect wasn't as deprived of ethnos as the Swiss Style but rather a blend of traditions with modernist design principles, creating unique and innovative works.

While early on, individual recognition was rare, over time, certain designers began to gain prominence and establish their identities as authors. The first notable figure, designers with name, face, and signature were fashion designers Aleksandar Joksimović and Mirjana Marić. They played crucial roles in this transition not just in fashion but in the entire design community.

Two state-owned giants Centrotextil and Jugoexport paved the way for Yugoslavia to emerge as a significant creator, producer, and exporter of fashion that reflected the country's unique socio-political context, cultural diversity, and artistic heritage. Centrotextil provided an opportunity to a young designer named Aleksandar Joksimović. He gained

TOP: BAZAR LOGO 1964. BOTTOM: BAZAR LOGO 1969. AUTHOR: ĐORĐE PRUDNIKOV.

popularity in his homeland following the creation of three masterful collections: *Simonida* (1967), *Stained Glass and Landscape,* and *Jerina* (1969). Unconventional for the era and the socialist regime, Joksimović's designs were inspired by medieval Byzantine clothing, traditional Serbian attire, and stained glass found in Orthodox and Catholic monasteries. These collections garnered attention in Western media, marking a significant shift in the perception of high fashion within socialist Yugoslavia. Subsequently, he received international acclaim and was hailed as the first haute couture designer from the Eastern Block.

In 1970, the French edition of Elle featured Joksimović's design on the cover, and the following year, he served as one of the judges in the Für Sie contest for the best graduating designer in Europe. Additionally, French magazine *L'Officiel* collaborated with Wool Bureau Inc. to produce a film on Joksimović's work and persona.

Later, he transitioned to prêt-à-porter, and his designs were distributed worldwide. Despite collaborating with various Yugoslavian design companies throughout his career, Joksimović never established his own label or worked under his name.

Aleksandar Joksimović also held the distinction of being the inaugural editor-in-chief of the oldest still-running fashion magazine in the region, *Bazar*. Established in 1964, according to the publisher's official statistics in 2024, has an average circulation of 33,000 copies. Despite being printed in Cyrillic, it continues to be sold throughout the entire former Yugoslavia, Western Europe, and the USA. With its header remaining unchanged for decades, *Bazar,* in a certain sense, preserves the memory of Yugoslavian fashion. However, two fashion designers revolutionized this for the entire design community— Joksimović became a household name, and Mirjana Marić became a pioneer in branding. Several years younger than Joksimović, Marić earned her degree from the Belgrade Faculty of Applied Arts and completed her Master's at the Royal College in London. Upon returning to Serbia, she began creating textiles and clothing for the industry, working for numerous companies across Yugoslavia, notably for the import-export giant Jugoexport. However, she later expanded her business beyond state borders and eventually lived and worked in the United States. Unlike Joksimović, she started signing and labeling her designs, becoming the first designer in Yugoslavia to do so.

MIRJANA MARIĆ LOGO VARIATIONS

Logo designs within the fashion industry of the SFRY encapsulated the intricate tapestry of the country's multifaceted history, position, and culture. These designs embodied a blend of the political context of socialist ideology, which varied over time, infused with cultural heritage and modernist principles, and influenced by international trends, particularly from the 1960s onwards.

Yugoslav logos offer a captivating glimpse into the interconnected realms of politics, culture, economy, and art within a socialist framework. Yugoslav designers navigated three languages and two alphabets, existing on the cusp of a deeply divided Cold War world. Personally, one of the most striking visual representations of effortlessly bridging this divide is the logo of Beko (Beogradska konfekcija). Its meticulously crafted letters allowed for simultaneous reading in both Cyrillic and Latin scripts. While undergoing various iterations and redesigns over the decades, the core concept remained intact.

In summary, the role of designers as authors in former Yugoslavia evolved from collective anonymity to individual recognition, influenced by the interplay of socialist ideology, cultural heritage, and international trends. Designers navigated the complexities of working in a multilingual, multi-ethnic environment while adhering to the state's political ideology. Their designs were results of multifaceted influences, intersecting geo-political position and rich heritage creating a unique blend and a lasting legacy that continues to shape the design landscape in the region today. This ancestry provides a distinctive lens through which to examine the role of design in molding national and cultural identities.*

I would like to thank Bojana Popović (Museum of Applied Arts, Belgrade), Koraljka Vlajo (Museum of Arts and Crafts, Zagreb), Ognjen Ranković (YugoLogo), Mario Leone Bralić, Lana Cavar i Narcisa Vukojević (Excavations: Signs of production, production of signs), and Lina Mihajlović (Bazar, Politika).
1 canadianarchitect.com/second-world-problems-yugoslavia-moma (17.6.2024)
2 YugoLogo.org

IAN LYNAM

THE BLOB OR A TALE OF TWO CITIES

IAN LYNAM works at the intersection of graphic design, design education and design research. He is faculty at Temple University Japan and operates the design studio Ian Lynam Design, the shop Sailosaibin and the Wordshape type foundry. Ian writes for IDEA (JP) and has published a number of books about design

PORTLAND, OREGON

It is the year 2000. I have gone back to college and am studying graphic design. I have also just finished one of the first freelance projects I've ever received as a designer. Knowing nothing about fashion other than just having met a nice guy who owned a screenprinting shop states away, I decided to start a streetwear brand with my financial windfall—the debut shirt featured a character which was a blob behind a DJ booth accompanied by some typography.

I have 100 shirts printed and three lone shops in Portland agree to carry them: a vintage clothing shop run by a friend, a record shop where my roommate is the record buyer, and another record shop where I don't know anyone.

The hiphop group Jurassic Five, one of my favorite musical acts came to town and their A&R rep purchases eight matching shirts for them to wear onstage from the vintage shop. I am given free tickets to the show and am invited to the backstage meet-and-greet with the band (which went really weirdly) but they group is graceful about it. They all wear my shirts onstage and I freak out—it is my entré to streetwear stardom—in my mind.

I go to bed a very happy young-ish man that night.

I receive a phone call the following day from the vintage shop. The morning after the Portland show, the band's roadie is tasked with doing laundry and washes the group's shirts soaked with sweat from an intense performance.

What washed out is not just the sweat, but the graphics as well.

My screen printer friend had not heat-cured the shirts properly and the Plastisol ink with which the graphics were printed just kind of glopped off all of them, ruining a load of laundry of a band that I really loved who were planning on wearing their coordinated shirts for the remainder of their West Coast tour.

I refund them for the shirts. I have to take the remaining shirts and ship them back to the screen printer to have them heat-set, which will take weeks due to shipping. The entire experience dashes my initial hopes about starting an apparel line, as I had accidentally stumbled into the best promotional situation I had ever seen in my life to date that week and the whole thing had melted into a literal blob.

I return to college with the hopes of finally getting an undergraduate degree. I study graphic design. I produce a handful more shirt designs and I make a bunch of miscalculations: notably that nobody wants certain sizes of shirts. I thought that I was being inclusive by making XL and XXL women's shirts. But nobody does. I am stuck with boxes of product that I cannot sell, much less give away, which I will drag around various American locales for a handful of years before donating all of it to a chain of thrift stores.

It is sad. I like designing apparel, but I don't have enough money to continue to pursue it. I graduate from college and then move to Southern California to pursue an MFA in graphic design. Two years later, I finish that and I scout far and wide for freelance clients, and I wind up designing a lot of apparel for major label music acts like KISS, Slipknot, System of A Down, Billy Fucking Joel, The Cult, The Beatles' estate, The Cars, Barbra Streisand, and at least fifty other musicians whose music I cannot stand.

It is weird. I am earning pretty good money designing apparel, but it feels really terrible because I am designing apparel for terrible musicians.

I design, produce and sell one more run of my own shirts around this time, a simple black T-shirt with the slogan "Portland is the new Brooklyn." just as the Portland gentrification boom was really kicking in. They all sell.

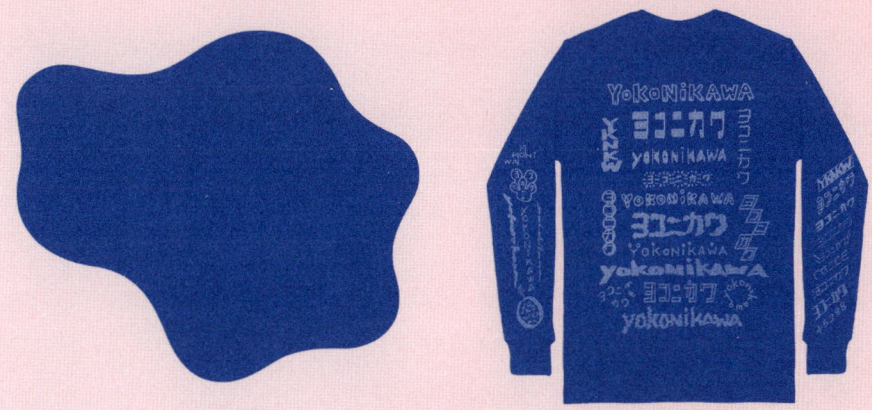

LEFT: BLOB. RIGHT: YOKONIKAWA MOTOCROSS SHIRT.

And then I give up on trying to design apparel. I work as an art director and designer at various agencies in Los Angeles, I move to Japan and work at various agencies as an art director and designer, and then I start teaching design. And throughout that whole time, I build up my own graphic design studio and run that for fifteen-plus years, aspiring for something more—something that I cannot put my finger on … something more than just the transactional nature of the designer / client model of capitalism.

TOKYO, JAPAN

It is 2021. There is a global pandemic occurring and my wife and I are aimlessly walking around Tokyo on one of the multitudes of aimless walks that we take over the course of said pandemic and we find a street with a beautiful park alongside it. And then we find a postage stamp-sized retail storefront on that street. And then we decide to open a shop there and we rent it.
We don't have any startup money. We don't have a business plan. My less than lofty aspirations for the space are that I will have a little bookshelf in the corner and that I will sell books that I was interested in. The rent is cheap enough that it doesn't matter if we make a lot of money or not. I suggest to my wife that it is basically an art project and something that we can devote ourselves to for the further remainder of the pandemic and maybe beyond if it actually works.
The problem with having a shop is that you have to sell shit. And we don't have a lot of shit to sell.
Moreover, we are stumped as to what to call this new venture. My wife asks me what I think of when I think of her. I reply "psilocybin," the naturally occurring drug in magic mushrooms that makes one hallucinate. I don't think she had ever heard the word before, but when I spell it out, we realize that this word is a non-starter for Japanese people trying to read the word in English because the spelling is so crazy. We spell it out phonetically, "S-A-I-L-O-S-A-I-B-I-N" and decide that this will be the name of the shop, as nonsensical as it is.
I design the identity for the shop—the name typeset in a typeface based on lettering from a painting by uptight Bauhaus student and Ulm co-founder Max Bill enclosed in a blob. For years, I had included this blob-shape in lectures at assorted design schools. I show students how the Bauhaus teacher Wassily Kandinsky had tried to report that all of human existence could be represented with a circle, and a triangle and a square, but that I felt like my life was more akin to a blob. The blob feels more like real life: the shape of an accident. A drip. A stain. A germ. An anomaly.

ZINE-AS-SHIRT-SHIRT

We make business cards and shop cards and stickers and seals and signage and a doormat and stamps and all these things with the type and the blob. And afterward, we make T-shirts in both long sleeve and short sleeve variations.

And we open our shop to the public in the middle of COVID-19. And people come, though at a trickle at first. We put up signage that says that only two people can be inside at a time. And the shirts that we make sell. The typographic things that we make are purchased by other human beings. We had picked pretty decent printers, and with the exception of one particular sweatshirt, the prints don't come off in the wash.

We have made a lot of apparel since then, including screen-printed garments, knitwear, scarves, blankets, shirts, pants, dresses, skirts. And so much more: pins, stickers, posters, bandanas, toys, zines-as-shirts, and most recently, type specimen socks. We've also figured out what we want to sell and what we want to be: a small shop that functions as a community space that encourages others to explore their own interests. Everyone is invited. Sailosaibin is a place that is subcultural without feeling attached to one particular subculture. The blob is just that: a blob. It transcends punk, rap, electro, hardcore, hip-hop, the small press, indie, metal, graphic design, art, and all of the other variegated colors of genre to meld them into something new that cannot be harnessed.

THE SAILOSAIBIN SHOP IN TOKYO, JAPAN

We have made a space that reflects and refracts who we really are: people living in the here and now with a sense of history, but just as much as sense of the future—and with all tenses, a space where typography lies at its nexus—both in books and on clothing. Typography is a thing that has to be learned. No one is born a natural typographer, just as no one learns to experience the world "correctly." Empathy is actually the same, though people prefer to ignore that—it is something learned most of the time.
And usually, neither comes out in the wash.

JIMMY HENDERSON

DON'T CALL IT A COMEBACK: THE RISE, FALL, AND RE-EMERGENCE OF CHAMPION

JIMMY HENDERSON is a designer, educator, and craft beer lover whose professional and teaching career have spanned more than a decade. His work and research focus on branding, packaging, logos, craft beer, and the human experience. He is currently teaching graphic design at Susquehanna University.

I remember with great fondness taking a Champion sweatshirt from my dad when I was younger. Oversized, comfortable, light gray with the script logo emblazoned across the chest, it became one of my favorite pieces of clothing at the time, and I kept it well into college. It had holes at a few seams and was tattered at the edges of the sleeves, but it was high quality and had held up for many years. Its minimalism was cool, straightforward, and bare-bones in branding, yet it didn't need anything else to stand out. I loved that sweatshirt—the thick fabric, the feel of it, and most importantly, the way it made me think of my dad.

Enter 2019, and I am in a mall in North Carolina and I happen to come across a new Champion store. A little surprised because I had not seen Champion ever sold this way, the logo is what caught my eye first, that instantly recognizable "C" with the script type mark and my reaction was almost visceral, excited even. I immediately thought of my old sweatshirt and the emotional attachment to the clothing and the logo was so powerful. I was drawn to it in a way I hadn't been with other sports brands I often frequented. Champion clothing filled the racks and seeing the logo used so many different ways in its own space was powerful. The sweat pants and shirts and classic reverse weave sweatshirts felt more modern and updated. It was a fresh look that still maintained its classic vibe at the same time. The type was still doing the heavy lifting as the script type mark proudly and boldly was splashed across the chest of sweatshirts, ran up the leg of joggers, or in some cases relied on just that "C" icon to sit playfully on the hip of a pair of shorts. I bought a pair of gray shorts with the "C" in vibrant red on the left leg and it felt right in a way that buying a pair of Nike or Jordan shorts never had.

The Champion story is inherently a tale of market domination that faded as fashion changed, sports apparel deals were rewritten, and staying power faded before erupting back on the scene as trends and style tastes cyclically came back around. A brand that has celebrated its 100th anniversary just recently, Champion and its trademark "C" icon and script type mark were synonymous with athletics and partnerships for decades at both the professional and college level of sports. The history of the brand and its heritage is well laid out on the company's website (Champion, n.d.) and speaks fondly of its creation and early history as a family owned business. Worn by the US Military, college sports teams (notably brand powerhouse Notre Dame for the first time in 1978), the NFL in the 1970s, and the 1992 Men's Olympic basketball team, Champion was known for high quality construction, durability, and the invention of the hoodie. Its timeless design and patented reverse weave sweatshirts could be found on every college campus, worn by musicians and celebrities, and was a staple of the sportswear style of clothing from inception and into the early 2000s. The simplicity of the designs, the weather resistant build of the clothing coupled with manufacturing techniques that prevented shrinking, and the brand power of the logo made Champion one of the most popular brands in the United States for decades as it touched every conceivable style and need of the market. Purchased by Sarah Lee in 1989 and peaking in the late 90s, the attention to the brand dwindled along with its offerings and its perception in the market shrank in the early 2000s as different divisions in the company were sold (Goulet, 2021, p. 17). Along side another popular sportswear brand in the 1990s, Starter, Champion slid into obscurity and began targeting a discount market. At this point it was largely viewed as a cheap clothing option that simply couldn't compete with flashier athletic brands. With Nike, Adidas, and Under Armour dominating the sports clothing market and snatching

CLASSIC CHAMPION SHORTS

up apparel contracts from some of the most recognizable sports brands in the country, Champion found itself on the outside looking in. The once powerful, American-made, sportswear company would need almost two decades, and being purchased by Hanesbrand in 2006, to find itself again and pivot back onto the scene.

The beauty of the Champion brand was always in its reliance on the strength and visibility of the logo. The "C" logo, introduced in 1956 (Champion, n.d.), was a staple of the brand and could be found on the left sleeve of every sweatshirt. Along with the script type mark, the logo design gave the brand so much versatility in how it was used on clothing. Being well balanced in size and shape lends to easy placement on any number of mediums from uniforms and tags to print and digital use. It's easy to design with and easy to design around but the confident feel of the logo allows it to do the heavy lifting in designing fashion looks for the Champion brand line of clothing. The bold red, white, and blue color scheme along with the logo design has remained unchanged for roughly 70 years, a hallmark of good logo design and incredibly important for a brand's staying power and recognizability in a crowded market. The custom letterform combines smooth rounded curves and sharp ends and works so well as a full color logo as well as in black and white. Size on clothing determines the vibe of those pieces as the "C" icon can be subtle and understated for a more classic look while increasing the size and splashing it across the chest or along a leg to allow the brand to be more vocal in how it is seen. It is a clear call back to the hip hop and skater scenes that adopted the brand in the 1980s and 1990s. Few brands can point to a logo as recognizable across multiple demographics and regions around the world as Champion which has always made its story so interesting and its fall from grace as equally difficult to understand.

But Champion was back. After a number of collaborations with new upstart clothing brands, Champion leaned into vintage nostalgia to anchor itself back into the fashion space. Champion leveraged type at the forefront along with a higher price tag to change the perception of the brand. The clothing has a way of taking you back and instead of pushing full tilt towards modernism like other brands it relied on the nostalgia of a classic athletic look that whispered football games in the snow, game days on Saturday, and basketball when the Dream Team exploded onto the scene and shocked the world. It felt like a new haircut on an old friend, a modern blend of old and new that multiple generations could wear side by side without feeling out of place. Even at the small Division III university where I teach graphic design the reverse weave gray sweatshirt with the Slab Serif university name spelled across the chest and that small iconic "C" on the sleeve was a familiar sight that tugged at feelings of the past. Champion hadn't ever left, it just went into the locker room down at the half and was looking for an inspirational speech to make that comeback we didn't know we missed but realized we wanted.

KYLIÈN BERGH, KARMEN SAMSON

HIJACKING THE SUPPORTER'S SCARF

COMMODIFYING IDENTITY AND THE CULTURAL JAMMING OF CONSUMER CULTURE

KYLIÈN BERGH is a researcher and practitioner in the field of graphic design. He is fellow at the Wim Crouwel Institute in Amsterdam (NL) and lecturer histories and theories of graphic design at the Royal Academy of Arts in The Hague, the Vrije Universiteit in Amsterdam and the University of Amsterdam. **KARMEN SAMSON** holds MAs in Fine Art and Design, and Arts and Culture. As a fashion practitioner and researcher, she aims to bridge the gap between theoretical research and practical application. Her work examines the symbiotic relationship between fashion and society, shedding light on how cultural developments influence fashion and vice versa.

*T*he stadium is packed. While tens of thousands of fanatics are chanting, forming a division of two opposing fronts, they are upholding a piece of knitwear. (FIG. 1) As far as the crowd is concerned, they are not just holding a piece of mechanically manufactured merchandise, but their engagement and support. But what is the role of the supporter's scarf in the spectacle of sport consumption, and how does it contribute to the notion of identity? What happens when the merchandise of the mass leisure ritual of sport consumption leaves the stadium?

When leaving the natural habitat of the stadium, the scarf is worn in public life and no longer restricted to the momentum of the sporting event. Like so, the attire of the mass ritual of sport consumption continues to signal allegiance, dedication, and support. While coming in a variety of shapes and sizes it always fits around the neck. Every neck. This makes it a highly inclusive and seemingly unisex fashion item, fulfilling the practical need of covering and protecting the neck—one of the most delicate parts of the human body. However, whereas sport fanaticism is often depicted as a masculine affair, knitwear, and the act of making it, is traditionally seen as a craft and associated with femininity. Despite one size fits all, there seems to be a constellation of gender connotations associated with the unisex object of the scarf.

In addition, the supporter's scarf seems to be tied to a specific subculture of sport fanaticism. However, through adaptation as merchandise for fashion and design practices, the medium becomes hijacked. Herewith, the supporter's scarf seems to bounce back and forth between various cultural categories, traditionally depicted as lowbrow or popular- and highbrow culture. In this way, it serves as an explicit form of cultural jamming. Yet how does this piece of mass consumption merchandise become the carrier of messages and identities? And what happens when design practices and activists hijack the medium?

LOCALIZING THE SCARF FROM KNITTING TO THE MACHINE

The threads of the supporter's scarf seem to date back to the congregation of the invention of mechanically producing knitwear in 1589, and its subsequent application as merchandise for the sport industry. Although football, and watching the games as a leisure activity, rose in popularity in Western Europe during the 19th century, the mass production and consumption of merchandise such as the replica kit would only develop throughout the 1970s.[1] Prior to this, the predominantly male sports spectators were dressed in their regular work or church day attire, as mid-century archival footage reveals. (FIG. 2) White-collared shirts, neckties, tweed jackets, dark overcoats, and hats overcrowded the arena. To showcase their allegiance and support, men occasionally wore colored ribbons, rosettes, or painted rattles.[2]

Initially, when the supporter's scarves entered the stadium, they were most often knitted by the same women who were encouraged to knit pullovers and scarves for their husbands and sons at the frontier during the Second World War. Such small-scale and individual acts of supportership changed due to the rising popularity of sport events. This coincided with the increasing media coverage, broadcasting the spectacle through the advent of color photography and television. As a result, color coding and merchandise alike formed the primary means to brand teams and differentiate between players. Eventually, the supporter's scarf evolved from hand-knitted pieces made by loving mothers into mass-produced merchandise manufactured by cold, hard machines.

FIG. 1: CHANTING FANS IN A FULL STADIUM, HOLDING UP THEIR FAN SCARVES
FIG. 2: SPECTATORS DRESSED IN THEIR REGULAR WORK OR CHURCH DAY ATTIRE, MID-CENTURY ARCHIVAL FOOTAGE

FIG. 3: THE SCARF—PARADOXELY ACTING AS AN IDENTITY SIGNIFIER MEDIATING BETWEEN THE SOCIAL AND THE SELF

MERCHANDISE AND THE MESSAGE: OBJECTS AND IDENTITIES

While gazing at the spectacle and mass ritual of sport consumption, the scarf materializes supportership into a tangible wearable artifact. Worn around the neck, the scarf, like a talisman, signifies a sense of belief and belonging. Through text, club crests, and foremost color—*par excellence the instruments of visual communication*—the knitted fabric forms a visible totem; a surface expressing identity.[3]

Herewith, the scarf carries the "expressive capacity" to "perform identity." This *expressive capacity,* as Ian Woodward describes in *Understanding Material Culture,* enables objects to articulate aspects of the self; for example, the engagement and interest of its carrier.[4] In the case of the supporter's scarf, it expresses the rooting for a favored team in particular, and a sense of belonging to like minded fanatics of the *soccer tribe* at large.[5] "In terms of personal identity," as Woodward writes, "objects *assist the credible, effective performance* of an identity—they are integral parts of an effective social performance whereby objects (seem to) fuse with their possessors in order to offer a convincing social performance."[6] As a social performance, the scarf derives its expressive capacity from the ritual of the gathering for the sport spectacle. It performs not as mere possessions, but rather as tokens of identities rooted in ritualistic and sacred-like leisure events.[7] Even outside the realm of the stadium, the scarf stands testimony of the community membership and thus continues the social performance of identification.

However, identification indicates a paradox of its own. Whereas the scarf performs the identity of the self, as means of distinction from others, it simultaneously ties the individual to a united community.[8] (FIG. 3.) Inevitably, the scarf inherits this paradox. As a medium transmuting club crests and colors it acts as an identity signifier mediating between the *social* and the *self*. What emerges from this intersection are cultural categories and collective identities. Despite its roots in the realm of soccer fandom, the scarf seems to fluctuate between a various array of cultural connotations and categorizations.

FIG. 4: THE SCARF AS A MEDIUM OF CRITIQUE AND SELF-EXPRESSION

THE SPECTACLE OF MASCULINITY IN SPORTS CULTURE

Scarves, from the perspective of football fanatics, flashes a sensation of masculinity, pride, and honor.[9] Within the walls of the stadium, the scarf becomes a hyperbolic tool to voice one's allegiance. Simultaneously, it propagates a masculine ethos, due to competitive urge provoking specific social expressive behaviors such as whistling, screaming, chanting, and scolding.[10] Football serves as a prime example showcasing how masculine traits and competitiveness—striving to assert dominance and superiority over one and another—are leveraged into the spectacle of sport consumption and its subcultures.[11] Sports inherently showcases rivalry and division—us against them, winners against losers. Within

FIG. 5: FEMINIST MOVEMENTS "LIBERATING" KNITTING AS A FORM OF AGENCY

this setting, the football scarf is both a symbol of glory, held high and proud in the sky, and a beacon of hope, clinging nervously in one's hands. At the heath of the moment, the football scarf is both a beacon of hope, clinging nervously in one's hands, as it is a symbol of glory, held high and proud in the sky. This transformation has made football more than just a competition for points; it has become a contest of dominance as well in which the scarf vocalizes status in the football ranks and serves as a token of masculinity.

DOMESTIC CRAFT OR FEMINIST AND ACTIVIST MEDIUM?

While the supporter's scarf connotes highly masculine sport fanaticism, its materiality and technique are predominantly associated with the hobby-like leisure activity of knitting and feminine crafts. Historically, women were responsible for managing the household and either acquiring or creating the necessary items for the family and household, including clothing. Accordingly, knitting as a transgenerational activity has significantly contributed to perpetuating the stereotype of women knitting in the domestic environment. This portrayal has played a crucial role in reinforcing gender roles and associated qualities like care, patience, and nurturing with femininity.

While stereotypes, often based on magnified assumptions found in reality, can have a belittling effect, it can also provide the means to hijack representations for the purpose of critique or self-expression. (FIG. 4.) Like so, feminist movements throughout the last two decades have increasingly adopted knitting to advocate their own political agendas.[12] Instead conforming to cultural stereotypes that constrain femininity, this approach "liberates" knitting as a form of agency resisting the patriarchy. (FIG. 5.) Such "craftivism" challenges rigid thinking and clichés associated with femininity, while also binding groups of women together, fostering collaboration, and providing mutual support.

CULTURAL JAMMING

The appearance of the supporter's scarf within the arsenal of fashion and design practices, as a medium channeling critical messages, hints at a form *of cultural jamming*.

FIG. 6: "PROTEST GEAR" BY THE ADAPT DESIGN DUO ADAPT RICHARD ASHTON AND JOSIE TUCKER

"Culture jamming, the act of resisting and re-creating commercial culture in order to transform society," as Jennifer Sandlin and Jennifer Milam describe in analyzing how pop and politics merge, "is embraced by groups and individuals who seek to critique and (re)form how culture is created and enacted in our daily lives."[13] By reverting the familiar language of advertising and mass media, cultural jamming uses consumer consciousness to critique consumer culture. Hijacking both the connotations of the supporter's scarf (as a populist object) and the recognizable vernacular aesthetics (as bold typography, contrasting color schemes, and the distinctive fringes), it re-charges the familiar medium with new *resistant* meaning.

Through this so-called *craftivism,* cultural jammers embrace a decentralized form of activism aimed at disrupting norms and instigating societal transformation. The intersection of femininity, affordability, and protest allows the scarf to adopt diverse roles and meanings. This versatility allows the explicit usage of the scarf as a wearable protest sign. While it is flexible, lightweight, compact, wearable, and resistant to damage—unlike the equivalent made of paper or cardboard—the scarf performs as a powerful protest utility. This is exemplified by "Protest Gear," created by the Adapt design duo Adapt Richard Ashton and Josie Tucker. (FIG. 6) Instead of advocating the mass ritual of sport consumption, they advocate environmental awareness by replacing club crests with messages such as "Climate Justice," "Fucx Your CO_2," and "Plant or Die."[14] Thus, the warm, cozy, soft, intimate, and delicate material of textile is being hijacked as a hyper political vehicle performing identification of counter culture, resistance and alternative community forming.

CONCLUSION

The simple rectangular stitches of knitted fabrics appear as a hyper diverse object; signaling not only a degree of dedication as a supporter's scarf, but also a sense of belonging. By transforming club crests and colors into wearable commodities, the scarf as a piece of merchandise for the mass consumption of sports, takes on the role of carrier of messages and identities. Whereas its natural habitat is set at the stadium's tribune, the supporter's scarf worn in daily life continues as a means of identification beyond the event of mass spectatorship. As an integral object in the identification of populist culture, it provides the medium for cultural jammers to hijack the object in order to convey different meanings or identities. Herewith it blurs distinctions between fashion—evolving around styles and wearable textile commodities—and visual communication as practices creating identities and messages through type and color. Even more so, it seems to bounce back and forth between a range of polarities, including feminine-masculine, highbrow-lowbrow, individual-collective, design-fashion. The hijacking of the supporter's scarf reveals the continuing tension between everyday culture and its critical questioning.

1 The kit refers to the standardized attire and equipment of professional football players. While this includes the shirt, socks and pants, it is the shirt in particular that forms a popular merchandise. This is mainly due to the fact that it is connected to individual icons; through the imprint of the player's name and number. The commercial exploitation of these reproductions as merchandise is known as "the replica kit."
2 Jeff McIntyre, *A History of Soccer Scarves explained*, accessed June 1st, 2024, ruffneckscarves.com/a/blog/a-history-of-soccer-scarves-explained
3 Approaching the scarf as a "visible totem" lends from Christopher Stride, Jean Williams, David Moor, and Nick Catley who analyze the replica kit as the most prominent display of the football club's color. See Christopher Stride, Jean Williams, David Moor, and Nick Catley, *From Sportswear to Leisurewear: The Evolution of English Football League Shirt Design in the Replica Kit Era*, Sport in History 35 (1, 2014): 156–94. doi:10.1080/17460263.2014.986518.
4 Ian Woodward, *Understanding Material Culture* (Los Angeles: Sage Publications, 2007), 134-5.
5 For an analysis of "the soccer tribe" see Desmond Morris, *The Soccer Tribe*, 1981.
6 Woodward, *Understanding Material Culture*, 137.
7 Christian Derbaix, Olivier Cabossart, and Alain Decrop, *Colors and Scarves: The Symbolic Consumption of Material Possessions by Soccer Fans*, Advances in Consumer Research 29 (2002): 513.
8 Ibid., 514.
9 Ibid
10 Ibid
11 Eduardo Archetti, *Soccer and Masculinity* in *The Argentina Reader: History, Culture, and Society*, ed. Gabriela Nouzeilles and Graciela R. Montaldo (Durham: Duke University Press, 2002), 521.
12 Harris, Anita, ed. *Next Wave Cultures: Feminism, Subcultures, Activism*. New York: Routledge, 2008. p. 7.
13 Jennifer A Sandlin and Jennifer L. Milam, "Mixing Pop (Culture) and Politics": Cultural Resistance, Culture Jamming, and Anti-Consumption Activism as Critical Public Pedagogy," Curriculum Inquiry 38, no. 3 (2008): 323. jstor.org/stable/25475909
14 Jenny Brewer, *Adapt launches Protest Gear, a football scarf-inspired collection emblazoned with activist slogans* It's Nice That, last modified November 4th, 2020. itsnicethat.com/news/adapt-protest-gear-scarves-fashion-graphic-design-041120

INTERVIEWS

CURIOSITY
QUESTIONS
ANSWERS
INSPIRATION
DOUBTS

2011

SLANTED × GOLNAR KAT-RAHMANI

GRAPHIC DESIGN, POLITICS, & FASHION

GOLNAR KAT-RAHMANI is a lecturer and typographer specializing in multilingual graphic design. As the founder and art director of Berlin-based Studio Katrahmani, she leads a team renowned for its expertise in typography, type design, visual identity, and editorial design.

Interview conducted by Julia Kahl.

TELL US A BIT ABOUT YOURSELF. HOW DID YOU GET INTO DESIGN?

GOLNAR KAT-RAHMANI: I grew up in Iran in a town about the size of Cologne called Sari. In my family and among the people around me, no one was educated in art or design or practiced it. There were more interests in literature, history, and other sciences.

Due to the extreme tensions between the new regime in Iran after the 1979 revolution and all Western powers (Europe and North America), Iran has been under very harsh sanctions from the outside. Additionally, the internal ideological politics banned cultural exchanges for more than two decades. Despite this, my parents did their best to provide us with access to books and cultural resources. I attended a state calligraphy school and spent two years learning calligraphy in the traditional way (calligraphy holds high traditional value in Iran, similar to China or Japan).

I have always loved drawing, often playing with the shapes of alphabets. At the time, I had no clue about the term "typography." I heard that word for the very first time when I was attending design classes to prepare for the university entrance exam for graphic design at the age of 17.

I used to study at a rigorous school in Iran, primarily for students excelling in mathematics. While completing my degree, I began preparing for the aptitude test for the art university.

AND THEN YOU STUDIED VISUAL COMMUNICATION IN IRAN?

G K-R: Yes, exactly. I studied visual communication at Tehran University, which had a more artistic approach and focused heavily on typography and poster design, with an emphasis on Swiss design.

Three years after I graduated, I decided to pursue a Master's degree and moved to Berlin, which was a tough decision for many reasons. I studied at Berlin Weißensee School of Arts for three years.

WHAT INSPIRES YOU MOST IN YOUR WORK?

G K-R: People and politics.

A major reason for this could be that, due to political circumstances, I was born in exile shortly after the Islamic Revolution. At that time, there was a massive wave of arrests of people with different views, and my parents' lives were in danger. When you grow up in Iran, even as a child, you think a lot about how to categorize the situations and understand what is actually happening around you. That had a very strong cultural influence on me.

Additionally, being surrounded by many amazing, strong, and kind souls who truly fought for a better Iran had a profound effect on me.

YOU ONCE SAID "THERE IS CURRENTLY AN EMOTIONALIZED REACTION WHEN LOOKING AT ARABIC CHARACTERS."

G K-R: Unlike Japanese characters, the reaction of viewers when looking at Arabic script is increasingly emotional today. The reception is influenced by various factors that have nothing to do with the script as an abstract sign system. Our perception and understanding are more than ever under the influence of social, political, and cultural developments. The rise of Islamic terrorism and its elevation to the central enemy of so called "Western culture," the political instability in the Middle East, the often difficult relationships among religions in daily coexistence, and increasing Islamophobia[1] have intruded into our daily consciousness. Viewers, influenced by a multitude of such media stimuli, no longer associate the Arabic-Persian letter and its script merely with exotic foreignness but increasingly with religion, politics, and perhaps even threat.

Reflecting on this automatic reflex reveals its cultural explosiveness. Prominent representatives of radical Islam, such as ISIS, strategically use this effect and deliberately stage Arabic script in a martial and war-like manner as part of a profound cultural struggle. This creates a negatively connoted typography and iconography of conflict and enemy, marginalizing the cultural value of a writing system.

HOW DO YOU SEE THE ROLE OF SCRIPT IN CULTURAL IDENTITY AND INTERCULTURAL EXCHANGE?

G K-R: I think it has a lot to do with the people you interact with and the social class you belong to. Many people communicate more with graphics than with text, while others convey content through written language. This makes it difficult to generalize. Script is a cultural asset that I have been working on intensively for a number of years because, in my eyes, it embodies more cultural identity than even the religions.

Most people are not fully aware of this. Over the last three decades, Persian and Arabic scripts have been strongly associated with negativ and hostile themes. Similar to the headscarf as a symbol of Islam, letters are also targeted. Our perceptions are increasingly influenced by social, political, and cultural tensions. The rise of Islamophobia has made Islam the number one public enemy of so-called Western culture, amidst political instabilities and wars in the Middle East, and religious conflicts in daily Western life.

All these factors contribute to Arabic-Persian script being seen as strange and exotic, often provoking negative feelings and marginalizing its cultural value. In contrast, Latin script is perceived positively in many parts of the world and is seen as high-quality, modern, and technologically advanced. For example, if a brand in Japan uses Latin characters, it is automatically perceived as more prestigious, and customers are often willing to pay twice as much for the goods or services. This is not due to the content but purely to the visual appearance of the font.

AND HOW SCRIPT IS PERCEIVED IS VERY DIFFERENT, DEPENDING ON HOW YOU ARE SHAPED.

G K-R: Exactly. I recently started working on typeface design for different corporate fonts again. I realized how important the small details are and how much they relate to cultural perceptions. Lately, I came across an Arabic script designed for a wide range of languages using this alphabet for various editorial contents from different countries. The designer made an innovative small change in dot shapes, following the Latin alphabets of the same typeface. The designer probably tried to transfer what is defined as modern or minimalist in Europe into the Arabic script. However, this did not work for some editorials and journalists as users. The customer did not find the visual appearance serious enough, so the script was not used as planned.

More than 900 million people around the world are confronted with Arabic script on a daily basis, be it on a linguistic or religious level. You simply have to realize that. Script does not play an overriding role in our everyday lives, as we currently have to deal with much bigger, more important issues in the world. Anthropologically and socially, however, it is extremely important.

AND THAT'S WHY YOU FOUNDED THE TYPE & POLITICS INITIATIVE? WHAT MOTIVATED YOU TO DO IT?

G K-R: That's right, I initiated the project about seven years ago and have been imparting my knowledge of Persian-Arabic scripts in workshops ever since, clearing up ideological prejudices. The trigger for this was probably a very personal experience. When I was relatively new in Berlin, I took the subway and often something to read in Persian in hand.

As I sat there, I noticed how I was being scrutinized and attracted the attention of strangers. However, it wasn't so much my appearance, as I was dressed in regular look and way in Berlin, but in combination with the Persian book (to them Arabic or Islamic) I made my counterparts feel a certain unease. They didn't know how to categorize me, there was no "label" for me. I wanted to do something about this partly unconscious discrimination and started to develop a few cards written a text in Arabic, Japanese and Devanagari (one of the Indian scripts), which I then made an experiment of people reactions to them and gathers their opinion and rapid emotions to them. Their reactions were very interesting and led to an initial discourse about it.

CAN I IMAGINE THE WORKSHOPS YOU OFFER AS PART OF THE INITIATIVE BEING SIMILAR?

G K-R: For the beginning, I share my knowledge from my research on Arabic-Persian script. What is it anyway? What does the script look like? What else can they see from the history of these scripts? The participants then experiment with non-Latin scripts and use them primarily as a tool. They are asked to look at the script neutrally, regardless of the stereotypical images they know. Most of them take great pleasure in the tradition of Persian writing and the unfamiliar aesthetics. At the same time, this is a platform for discourse, which is unfortunately still in its infancy, because there is so little knowledge available, so little known, that I often have to start from scratch in my workshops.

WHAT DO YOU THINK NEEDS TO BE CHANGED IN TEACHING AT UNIVERSITIES SO THAT ARABIC SCRIPT, OR NON-LATIN SCRIPT IN GENERAL, IS DE-EXOTICIZED?

G K-R: Same as many I also believe that the perspective on this must be fundamentally changed. Social media is already helping to make students much more open to other writing systems these days.

Last year, I started formulating a pedagogical concept for a new term in German design academic schools called "Intercultural Design Wissen in Praxis." I am already in contact with some professors about this. So far, I have been able to hold a week-long workshop on this term with a focus on Intercultural Typography in Poster Design at Burg Giebichenstein School of Art in Halle. It may be enough to deal intensively with non-Latin scripts once during your studies to develop a different attitude, a different interest, and a different perspective. To achieve this, it is important to do intensive research and to engage with the subject. It is also a realization for students that during research, you often only find digitized material from North America and Europe. It is not nearly as easy to find materials when the subjects are from non-Western European countries. I think this whole process, including the difficulties encountered during the research, is very important as part of learning new perspectives of the real world out there.

WHAT MOTIVATED YOU TO PRINT TYPOGRAPHIC, NON-LATIN DESIGNS ON TEXTILES?

G K-R: My goal with the *Type & Politics* project has always been to promote better living together and acceptance in the societies we live in. *Type & Politics* supports this goal by presenting Arabic-Persian script in a new context to challenge negative connotations and labels.

The project showcases these scripts' other capacities, demonstrating that they can also be funky, funny, or stylish. By looking at them detached from negative associations, one can appreciate their beauty. I often work with screen printing on textiles because it creates a mobile poster in the city, accessible to everyone, not just a special audience in gallery rooms.

An outfit then becomes a moving poster in the cityscape.

AT FIRST GLANCE, THE SCRIPT IS NOT ALWAYS IMMEDIATELY RECOGNIZABLE AS SUCH, ESPECIALLY FOR THOSE WHO ARE NOT FAMILIAR WITH ARABIC OR PERSIAN SCRIPT. IT COULD ALSO BE PERCEIVED AS A GRAPHIC PATTERN.

G K-R: For my Namak-e Safar collection, I worked exclusively with Qudratkufi, a script from the 12th century mainly used in Iran for building inscriptions. It is very typical for Iran and is also used in writing poetry. What I really liked about it is its linearity and the geometric shapes it consists of, such as squares, rhombuses, and rectangles. It has a unique look that resonates with the visual taste of designers or people in this part of the world—an international language of forms.

You won't find any translations on the textiles because I want people to talk about it if they are interested. I believe these letters are as diverse in their appearance as the people from the Middle East living here. Just as we do not have visual translations of our looks, these letters or outfits also shouldn't, yet they can still be accepted. Like getting to know foreign faces or persons, these typographies on outfits require interest and communication, which I believe is the key.

The name of the collection has something to do with migration. "Safar" means "journey" and "Namak" means "salt." You could translate it as "taste of the journey." The motifs show the names of Middle Eastern cities, where the Arabic alphabet originated, and their distances in kilometers to Berlin. The concept is flexible, allowing you to choose any city from the Middle East and any destination worldwide to create your individual outfit.

This collection offers a taste of a different Middle East, one that the world often only associates with war and religious conflicts. It is for those unfamiliar with this look and alphabet, for feeling and learning as a way of understanding, and for joining different worlds based on a mutual interest in typography.

TO WHAT EXTENT DO YOU SEE A CONNECTION BETWEEN SCRIPT AND POLITICAL MESSAGES OR SOCIAL MOVEMENTS?

G K-R: Graphic design has a significant impact on social movements. All posters in demonstrations—typography, illustrations, colors, and much more. Depending on how you use letters, colors, and aesthetics, you can evoke different feelings and purposes. In demonstrations, graphic design plays an important role in a direct communication. You can also observe these effects in political graffiti or wall-writings, especially in countries like Iran, suffering under the dictatorships. All those new political "call to actions" on social media are another obvious proof of it.

WOULD YOU SAY THAT WITH THE FASHION AND THE PROJECTS YOU DO, YOU "DEPOLITICIZE" ARABIC OR PERSIAN SCRIPT TO A CERTAIN EXTENT?

G K-R: My opinion on this is: "everything is political," because we instinctively have to judge everything—everything that happens is based on some kind of decision we make. Sometimes it just helps to put a spotlight on a certain topic and that's what I try to do with types on my fashion.

THANK YOU VERY MUCH!*

* For more of Golnar Kat-Rahmani projects, see pages 110 / 111.
1 Islamophobia is a misnomer since phobia implies an innate fear, whereas the correct term for it would be "Islamfeindlichkeit" in German or "ستیزی اسلام" in Persian

SLANTED × MIRKO BORSCHE

EVERYONE'S DOING SOCCER JERSEYS NOW

MIRKO BORSCHE is a renowned German graphic designer, art director, and the founder of Bureau Borsche. Since 2007, he has served as the creative director at *Zeit Magazine.* His studio seamlessly navigates between diverse realms, including corporate clients, luxury fashion brands, and the experimental art scene. Bureau Borsche notably revamped The Face and brought a bold aesthetic to the Bavarian State Opera. Additionally, the studio has established a strong presence in the fashion and football worlds, collaborating with brands like Nike, Supreme, and Balenciaga, as well as football clubs such as Inter Milan, Venezia FC, Athens Kallithea FC, and Young Boys Bern. These collaborations illustrate a growing trend where football intersects with fashion.

Interview conducted by Lars Harmsen.

IN 2019, YOUR DESIGN EXPERTISE WAS APPLIED TO THE VENICE PAVILION'S IDENTITY DURING THE BIENNALE, WHICH HAD THE THEME OF "FAKE NEWS." HOWEVER, THIS STRONG ASSOCIATION WITH VENICE DID NOT DIRECTLY LEAD TO YOUR WORK WITH VENEZIA FC, CORRECT?

MIRKO BORSCHE: No, the two projects were independent of each other. Years ago we worked on a project for Nike. When a consultant from that project moved to Inter Milan, he brought us along because he was excited about what we were doing. The connection with Venezia FC came about differently. The club had just been bought by an American, Duncan L. Niederauer, who brought in an American agency for advice. One of the agency's owners had previously worked for Supreme, and since we also collaborate with Supreme, that's how the connection was made. At that time, both Inter and Venezia were in Serie A, but on very different levels—Inter was a world-class club, while Venezia had just been promoted and was relatively unknown. When we started working with them, Venezia had about 7,000 followers on social media; today, they have over 350,000.

IT SEEMS THAT FASHION REALLY TAKES THE CENTER STAGE, PARTICULARLY WITH VENEZIA. WHEN I WAS IN VENICE, I NOTICED THE POSTERS ANNOUNCING THE MATCHES—THEY HAD A VERY FASHION-LIKE APPEARANCE. EVEN THE JERSEYS SEEM TO STRONGLY EXPRESS THIS BLEND OF TYPOGRAPHY AND FASHION. HOW MUCH OF A ROLE DID YOU PLAY IN GIVING VENEZIA THIS FASHIONABLE LOOK?

There's definitely a jersey hype in fashion right now. Brands like Louis Vuitton, Balenciaga, and Stussy are all making soccer jerseys. When we started, soccer jerseys weren't considered fashionable; people might buy old jerseys from the '90s or 2000s, but there wasn't much interest in contemporary ones. Our work with Venezia wasn't initially aimed at the fashion scene, but the club asked us to redesign their look, including the jerseys. At that time, they had no sponsor and very little money, even though they were in Serie A. We suggested creating jerseys that were simple and old-school, with "Venezia" prominently displayed on the front. We also partnered with the City of Venice, allowing us to open two shops in the city. The idea was that tourists could bring home a unique souvenir—a fashionable soccer jersey. The whole concept took off, and the fashion industry noticed. Over the years, we've continued to build on that success, which is how the slogan "The World's Most Fashionable Club" came to be.

WITH YOUNG BOYS, IS THE APPROACH SIMILAR TO WHAT YOU DID WITH VENEZIA, OR ARE THERE SIGNIFICANT DIFFERENCES?

The approach is similar in some ways, but there are differences. For Young Boys, we focused on the club's history and the unique characteristics of Bern. The logo itself is beautifully designed with elegant typography, which is unusual for a sports team. We took inspiration from Bern's Zytglogge clock tower, incorporating elements like the clock's battlements and Roman numerals into the jersey design. The response from the fans has been overwhelmingly positive, and we're now releasing a second jersey with a theme based on the Aare river that flows through Bern. This one has a totally different, almost hippie vibe.

WHAT KIND OF JERSEY WILL THAT BE?

It's going to be a warm-up jersey that the players wear before the game. We first explored this concept with Venezia. Warm-up

LEFT: VENEZIA FC PRE-MATCH JERSEY. RIGHT: ATHENS KALLITHEA FC 23/24 JERSEY

jerseys existed before, but they were usually standard designs from Nike or Adidas. We decided to create something more distinctive. For example, with Venezia, we designed warm-up jerseys in the club's three colors—orange, green, and black—which resonated well with the fans. Young Boys wanted to collaborate with us late in the season, so we suggested making a warm-up jersey that would be as beautiful as a home jersey but without the constraints of sponsor logos. This allowed us more creative freedom, and the result was a stunning, detailed jersey with glossy prints and intricate embossments.

PALM ANGELS IS ANOTHER PROJECT YOU'RE INVOLVED IN. COULD YOU TELL US MORE ABOUT YOUR TYPOGRAPHIC WORK FOR THEM?

Francesco Ragazzi, the chief designer and owner of Palm Angels, used to work at Moncler, and we still collaborate with him on Moncler projects. Similar to Supreme, Palm Angels uses a lot of monograms and graphics. Over the years, we've worked on various projects, from simple T-shirt graphics to collaborations like the Moncler partnership with Haas and Palm Angels.

Typography has become increasingly dominant in our work, especially with brands under the New Guards Group, like Off-White. Our redesign of Balenciaga's typography was a significant turning point, leading to its widespread use in high fashion.

WHAT'S PARTICULARLY INTERESTING ABOUT SUPREME IS HOW THEY ADOPTED BARBARA KRUGER'S VISUAL STYLE. HOW DOES YOUR COLLABORATION WITH SUPREME WORK?

Supreme's adoption of Barbara Kruger's style was genius—it's a blend of street culture and art. Our collaboration with them is straightforward; we often get requests to create new T-shirt graphics or collections based on specific themes, like the legendary Cross-Box logo, which was our design. Sometimes, we're asked to design a collection for a specific store opening, like in Berlin or Milan. Each project is unique, but the process is always collaborative and market-oriented.

THANK YOU!*

* For more of Mirko Borsche's projects, see pages 98/99.

SLANTED × UCON ACROBATICS
SMUDA & FUSSENEGGER

MINIMALISM CONTRIBUTES TO SUSTAINABILITY

UCON ACROBATICS blends creative design with sustainability, offering timeless products that transcend seasonal trends. Committed to minimal design and minimal emissions, the brand ensures quality without compromising on ethics—respecting people, animals, and the environment. Rooted in Berlin's creative scene and driven by artist collaborations, Ucon Acrobatics provides high-quality, durable designs for a new generation of forward-thinking creatives.

Interview conducted by Julia Kahl.

210

JOCHEN, YOU FOUNDED UCON ACROBATICS IN 2001 TOGETHER WITH MARTIN. HOW DID THAT COME ABOUT? WHAT IS YOUR BACKGROUND?

JOCHEN SMUDA: That's right, Martin and I started Ucon Acrobatics during a period when we were deeply involved in the skate scene. This was right before we started studying. Some friends were launching their own basic skate labels, which inspired us. We began with the classic approach of printing T-shirts in a friend's basement and selling them at events. Over time, our brand evolved from skate apparel to streetwear to street fashion, and eventually to accessories. Time has gone by incredibly fast. Around 2016, we shifted our focus towards bags and backpacks and began incorporating sustainable materials with bottle recycling. Managing online sales and returns is much simpler with accessories compared to clothing.

WHAT DOES YOUR TEAM LOOK LIKE, HOW ARE THE TASKS DISTRIBUTED?

JS: We're a small team, spread out across Berlin and Vienna, with contributors in other parts of Europe. Most of our work is done online, with around ten people involved. Until three years ago, it was just three of us, but as the brand expanded internationally, we brought more people on board. Most markets we handle through agents and distributors. Over the years, we've optimized our processes significantly, always aiming for efficiency and lean operations. We did all the tasks in a company ourselves for a long time before we decided to outsource them to external partners, so we know what is essential.

YOU JUST MENTIONED OPTIMIZATION— YOUR BAGS AND BACKPACKS ARE VERY MINIMALIST IN TERMS OF DESIGN, ALTHOUGH VERY FUNCTIONAL. IS AESTHETICS ALSO PART OF THIS PHILOSOPHY?

MARTIN FUSSENEGGER: From the beginning, we've aimed for a symbiosis of design and minimalism. Minimalist concepts haven't really changed that much over time. Eye opening for me as a teenager was to see works of the graphic designer Otl Aicher and Dieter Rams. They were a major influence on my decision to study product and graphic design. "Design as little as possible," and "Form follows Function" is still in the DNA of our brand. This approach influenced our clothing line and continued then with our accessories. Many people try to get rid of goods which have no meaning to them. Often they notice that the products they want to keep are the ones which have a minimalistic approach. It avoids being fashionable and therefore never appears antiquated. Minimalism contributes to sustainability—and also saves money. This is also an important aspect for us.

YOU JUST MENTIONED THE COLLABORATION WITH ARTISTS. WHAT IS YOUR STRATEGY, OR HOW DO YOU SELECT THE ARTISTS? HOW DOES THE COLLABORATION COME ABOUT?

MF: We see our bags and backpacks as the perfect canvas that is carried on the streets. We select artists whose work appeals to us, rather than the "minimalist approach." We continue to work with illustrators and designers that we think are cool and have a unique approach, regardless of their level of popularity or reach. Of course, we also collaborate with well-known artists like Eike König. Upcoming collaborations with Studio Feixen and Fons Hickmann are examples of projects we're excited about.

IS IT THE CASE THAT YOU ALWAYS PRODUCE A LIMITED NUMBER OF THESE COLLABORATIONS OR DO YOU ALSO PRODUCE MORE? HOW CAN ONE IMAGINE THAT?

JS: It varies. Sometimes we use a royalty fee model, allowing us to extend the production if the items sell quickly. For collaborations like for Bauhaus Shop, we agree on a fixed quantity, and once it's sold out, that's it. Most of these limited editions sell out, with only a few pieces left.

THAT ALSO HAS SOMETHING TO DO WITH SUSTAINABILITY IF YOU PRODUCE QUANTITIES THAT SURVIVE. HOW DO YOU SEE IT, DOES SUSTAINABILITY PLAY A COMPLETELY DIFFERENT ROLE IN THE MINDS OF CONSUMERS TODAY THAN IT DID 10 YEARS AGO?

JS: When we started using recycled PET for our backpacks in 2015, the market wasn't ready. Acceptance was challenging and many retailers were skeptical. Since then the awareness and demand for sustainable products have increased. It has become a critical marketing topic and addressing the environmental impact of our overconsumption. However, this year we see the challenge that consumers are once again turning to less sustainable products that are slightly cheaper due to the general rise in costs.

I READ THAT THE TEXTILE AND CLOTHING INDUSTRY IS RESPONSIBLE FOR 10% OF GLOBAL CO_2 EMISSIONS. I THINK VERY FEW PEOPLE ARE AWARE OF THAT.

JS: It's alarming. Every second, a truckload of textile waste is incinerated somewhere in the world, with less than 1% being recycled. The fashion industry is one of the least sustainable industries on the planet and we want to raise awareness about that and educate consumers. Unfortunately, greenwashing by big brands has eroded trust. We have to go deep into the processes and unravel this and improve our processes continuously. It's crucial for the future of our industry to take responsibility and push for genuine sustainable practices that are already available on the market.

I WOULD LIKE TO RETURN TO THE SUBJECT OF CIRCULAR TEXTILE ECONOMY. HOW DOES IT WORK?

MF: The textile industry must establish its own functioning waste recycling instead of buying up bottles from the food industry because it is cheaper. There are different approaches to reach a circular textile economy. Just like plastic bottles, uncolored textile waste can also be mechanically recycled into new material as long as it is made of 100% PET. However, this is almost only the case with scraps from the textile industry. For post-consumer textiles there is often a mix of materials. One process that could change the textile industry from the ground up is chemical recycling, since it only needs an input with 85% material purity. In our case, this means we need to have textiles with <85% polyester and >15% other fibers e.g. cotton. The higher the material purity, the less energy is needed for chemical recycling. Our aim is therefore to manufacture products with almost 100% recycled mono-materials from our own industry, which can then be recycled again and again. This creates a cycle.

WHAT ARE THE CHALLENGES OF MAKING FASHION SUSTAINABLE? THERE IS CERTAINLY A MARKET FOR IT, BUT HOW DO YOU MANAGE TO CONVINCE PEOPLE OUTSIDE THE "SUSTAINABILITY BUBBLE" OF RECYCLED MATERIALS? HOW DO YOU ENVISION UCON ACROBATICS' ROLE IN THE FUTURE OF SUSTAINABLE FASHION?

MF: Designing circular products requires not just an extra step in the process, but an entirely new approach. Every design decision affects the circularity of a product. In the shift from a linear to a circular economy, all components—from materials to fabric treatment—must undergo a review based on the criterias of reduced environmental impact, longevity and recyclability.

JS: Small companies have the advantage of agility. If we think a measure makes sense, we implement it as quickly as possible. There's no need for months of meetings and feasibility studies. In this case, however, we made the decisions based on ecological rather than financial considerations. For instance, Martin has dedicated

LEFT: LOTUS SERIES CAMPAIGN. RIGHT: HALF CUT HAJO MINI BACKPACK.

several months on-site with our producers, collaborating with around 30 partners—from yarn manufacturers to sewing factories—to find innovative solutions with the least impact on the environment. At the same time, we have put the issue of textile recycling on the agenda with downstream partners in the supply chain and established business relationships between manufacturers so that others can follow this path more easily. We want to take a pioneering role and hope for imitators. If larger brands take notice and begin to adopt similar practices, it would be a significant step forward for the industry.

ONE LAST QUESTION: DO YOU HAVE A FAVORITE PRODUCT?

JS: That changes from time to time. We design products for everyday life—items we personally find essential. Currently we focus on bike backpacks, as many of us frequently commute by bike. These backpacks are perfectly suited for daily use, being waterproof, highly reflective, and equipped with magnetic buckles and fasteners. We are proud of the fact that we really enjoy using the products we make, manufactured from our own developed materials.

I AM A BIG FAN OF YOUR BAGS. THANK YOU VERY MUCH!

SLANTED
× JEAN-BAPTISTE LEVÉE

AS EXPERTS, OUR ADVICE MATTERS

JEAN-BAPTISTE LEVÉE has designed over a hundred typefaces for industry, moving pictures, fashion and media. He is the founder of the independent foundry Production Type, a digital type design agency founded in 2014 in Paris, with offices in Paris and Shanghai. Initially a two-person operation, it has grown into a small business with 10 employees. While their work in custom type design for luxury, fashion and media sectors and retail catalogue development remains consistent, the company has expanded its focus to include broader aspects such as communication, long-term art direction, and licensing philosophy. The foundry promotes diversity among its team, aiming to offer contemporary typefaces to design professionals.

Interview conducted by Lars Harmsen.

WHEN WAS THE LAST TIME YOU WENT SHOPPING FOR CLOTHES?
JEAN-BAPTISTE LEVÉE: Last month? Let me think ... Yes! Last month, in a store.

YOU LAUNCHED PRODUCTION TYPE (PT), BUT FIRST, YOU CALLED YOUR COMPANY BAT (BUREAU DES AFFAIRES TYPOGRAPHIQUES). CAN YOU GIVE US A BRIEF RECAP OF YOUR PROFESSIONAL JOURNEY?
J-B L: I started out as a freelancer for about ten years. Then, in 2008, I co-founded BAT with three other partners. Four years later, in 2012, I left the operational management of the foundry. In 2014, I opened PT. Then, in 2016, I bought BAT from my former partners and merged its catalog with PT's. Today, BAT no longer exists, and all its assets are held by PT.

YOUR MOTHER WAS A TEACHER, AND YOUR FATHER WORKED AS A POSTMAN. IS IT THANKS TO THEM THAT YOU BECAME A TYPOGRAPHER?
J-B L: When I say that, it's more of a joke. My life revolves around letters. Typography is a natural extension of art studies. But indeed, from the age of six or seven, I asked to take drawing and painting classes, and that continued without stopping. My parents never opposed it; they actually encouraged it, even though they didn't come from an artistic background. It gave me a more literature-based cultural approach, as is common in France.

YOU'VE DESCRIBED YOUR FOUNDRY AS DESIGNING "USEFUL TYPE WITH AN EDGE." HOW DO YOU CHOOSE THE FONTS YOU DESIGN?
J-B L: There's a dual flow that might seem contradictory, almost like a dichotomy, but it's actually very coherent. It's for both the typefaces I design, the ones we create internally as a team, and those we integrate from external sources into PT's catalog. The typefaces must logically expand the catalog's expressive capabilities, without having fifty grotesques. Candidate typefaces must also be compatible with the existing design flow and the PT catalog overall. I see the catalog as a continuous stream that each new typeface must enrich. Sometimes it's tough to decide. We often get proposals, and we have to say, "Sorry, we already have something similar, so we won't weaken the catalog by adding it." Sometimes, we also have to say, "Sorry, but PT isn't the right place for certain designs because they're too decorative, too historical, too tame, etc." We're looking for designs that balance all these aspects without excess. That's what "useful type with an edge" means—typefaces with a strong pre-artistic stance that doesn't interfere with usability. Balancing the two is challenging.
In custom typefaces, we often respond to client requests. The client's demand is always the same: something that reflects the brand's ethos and is ownable. We try to position ourselves as experts rather than mere providers. As experts, our advice matters—it's not just an opinion but a visual recommendation for the benefit of a brand, product, service, or company. Simply fulfilling client requests is not enough. At PT, we strive to contribute more to the discussion than just what is asked.

PT WAS COMMISSIONED TO DESIGN THE NEW CUSTOM TYPEFACE FAMILY FOR LVMH, THE GLOBAL LEADER IN LUXURY PRODUCTS. LVMH SOUGHT A TYPOGRAPHIC VOICE THAT WOULD BE COMFORTABLE ON STATIONERY, ON-SITE COMMUNICATIONS, AS WELL AS IN LOGOS AND SIGNATURES. IS THAT POSSIBLE? HOW?
J-B L: LVMH, with its financial value and global presence, is huge. But it's still a holding company with holding activities. When we worked on the typography, LVMH was aware of its status as a holding company

LVMH Air ExtraLight
LVMH Air ExtraLight Italic
LVMH Air Light
LVMH Air Light Italic
LVMH Air Regular
LVMH Air Italic
LVMH Air Bold
LVMH Air Bold Italic

Christian Dior
COUTURE

TOP: LVMH CUSTOM TYPEFACE FOR LVMH. BOTTOM: LOGOTYPE FOR CHRISTIAN DIOR COUTURE.

and wanted to transform both its operational approach and its public image. Their goal was to organize public events like "Les Journées Particulières," open house events, and award ceremonies like "Innovation for Presence" and for promoting women in high-value intellectual professions. These activities are traditional at their core and more like foundation activities, but atypical for a holding company. The perceived image also involved opening up to the public. So, in many ways, it was more like client relations work, directly from LVMH to the public, rather than from the LVMH brands to the public. This gave us much more interest in intervening typographically than if it were just for a holding company, where our response would be to use an existing catalog typeface adapted for them.

WAS IT AN ART DIRECTOR FROM LVMH WHO PUT YOU IN COMPETITION WITH OTHER TYPE FOUNDRIES, OR HOW WAS THE REQUEST MADE?

J-B L: We don't do competitions. That's the advantage of being well-known. The relationship began with the design agency responsible for LVMH's visual identity redesign (Cake Design, led by Thibaut Mathieu) and then with LVMH's communications department. I knew they had done some research to understand how type design works, trying to be good clients—those who are interested in the subject and can articulate their needs well. When LVMH and Cake Design approached us, they had a well-formulated and interesting request, which isn't always the case. We could sense that there was room for us to offer expert opinions, which was confirmed over time. We increasingly accompanied the client as advisors, while also keeping space for artistic expression. It was a tremendous privilege to work with a client of this caliber. We interacted with very cultured and knowledgeable people.

The relationship was extremely enjoyable, as we could delve deeply into typographic culture, presenting things in a reasoned manner rather than just pedagogically. We worked in the way I prefer, which is to describe what we do—saying what we do and doing what we say. With them, we could go very deep into the nuances, details, and references, which was appreciated then and continues to be. We remain in contact, and the world benefits when you have clients of this quality.

I'M A BIG FAN OF COURRÈGES, KNOWN FOR ITS MINIMALIST DESIGNS FROM THE 1960S INFLUENCED BY MODERNISM AND FUTURISM. WHAT WAS YOUR PROJECT FOR THIS ICONIC FASHION BRAND?

J-B L: Courrèges is one of those projects we enjoy because it's very refreshing. We worked for Courrèges around 2016 with design director Jean-Baptiste Talbourdet and fashion art director Lolita Jacobs. At that time, the fashion art directors had just changed, signaling a typographic reboot as well. It wasn't the first time we worked with Jean-Baptiste Talbourdet, so we already had a good working relationship, meaning a shared vocabulary, understanding of expectations, requests, and ways of working.

Jean-Baptiste knew our methods, our process, and what to expect from us, while also knowing we could surprise him. We developed a typeface, a single style, that bridged the gap between clothing labels, the clothes themselves, and advertising campaigns, including the logo. Unfortunately, it wasn't a long-lived typeface, as Courrèges has seen changes in art directors, each wanting to make their mark. But it's possible the typeface might reappear soon.

YOU WORK FOR DIOR, VUITTON, AND CARTIER. IS THERE AN ANECDOTE ABOUT THESE MAJOR FRENCH LABELS THAT YOU'D LIKE TO HIGHLIGHT IN THIS INTERVIEW?

J-B L: The privilege we have in France is the sheer number of premium or luxury brands. What I've learned from working with these brands is that they don't just buy a service; they buy a result. This keeps us in the position of experts, not just service providers who deliver on a request. You can find typefaces at all levels of seniority, pricing, and budgets, but these brands aren't interested in that. They're interested in the value creation that comes from expertise.

These brands know typography much better than one might think and recognize its value-creating potential. When they come to us or other colleagues who work in fashion and luxury, they know they're seeking a promise of added value. It's very rewarding for the industry, in contrast to the more superficial requests like "I need someone to make a font, I don't know how to use the software," which can be detrimental.

AND ONE LAST QUICK QUESTION: DURING OUR ZOOM INTERVIEW, YOU WERE IN A CAR. YOU DID THE BRAND LOGO FOR RENAULT ALPINE. DID YOU GET A CHANCE TO TAKE IT FOR A SPIN?

J-B L: Yes, of course! It's like a little toy—you're sitting in a light, super-maneuverable little jet fighter. It's very, very enjoyable, a real pleasure.

THANK YOU!*

* For more of Jean-Baptiste Levée's projects, see pages 98/99, 131/132.

APPENDIX

INDEX
WWW
INSTA
COLOPHON
IMPRINT

205TF, FRA @205tf 205.tf	129, 130	**MIRKO BORSCHE /** **BUREAU BORSCHE, DEU** @bureauborsche bureauborsche.com	084 085 I, p. 207	**FLORIAN ENGELHARDT, DEU** @emgelhardt	002
29LETTERS TYPE **FOUNDRY [29LT], ESP** @205tf 205.tf	131, 132	**SARAH BROECKER, DEU** @sbroecker_	115	**ESTUDI TONI BAUZÀ, ESP** @estuditonibauza estuditonibauza.com	023
40MUSTAQEL, EGY @40mustaqel 40mustaqel.com	095	**SOLEDAD GALLARDO /** **BURBUSH DESIGN, ESP** @burbush_design soledadgallardo.com	064	**DUOLIN FANG, USA** @bleakyogurt	021
GIANLUCA ALLA, **NICOLETTA BELARDINELLI /** **AGOF, GBR** @agof.design a-g-o-f.com	117	**CHAE BYUNGROK / CBR,** **KOR** @chae_byungrok chaebyungrok.com	026	**DENNIS FECHNER, BEL / DEU** @dennis_fechner dennisfechner.de	019
AMORE STORE, DEU @amorestoreberlin AMORESTORE.DE	057	**SOPHIA CARLONI, DEU** @sophia.carloni sophiacarloni.de	090	**BORBALA FERENCZ, HUN** @b_o_r_b_a_l_a_ ferenczborbala.com	017
APPEAR OFFLINE, HRV @appear___offline appear-offline.com	079	**VALENTINA CASALI, ITA** @typophrenic ypophrenic.com	086 087	**IOANNIS FETANIS, GRC** @fetanisioannis_dw fetanisioannis.com	016
MAKSIM ARBUZOV, **MNE** @maksimarbuzov maksimarbuzov.com	109	**ANNIJA ČESKA, AUT** @annijaceska annijaceska.com	088	**JONAS FISCHER, DEU** @jns_fschr jonas-fischer.design	058
KITTI BAKONYI, HUN @kittkedesign	025	**SHIN-HEE CHIN, USA** @shinheechin shinheechin.com	011	**LAURA LE GAL, FRA** @lauraleg__al	054
BEIERARBEIT, DEU @beierarbeit beierarbeit.de	092	**CK MAURER, DEU** @ai_made_me_do_this ck-maurer.com	020	**LOUISA GRAMBOLE, DEU** @sleepwalk_souvenirs sleepwalksouvenirs.de	050
WALTER VAN BEIRENDONCK, **BEL** @waltervanbeirendonckofficial waltervanbeirendonck.com	C 075	**AURÉLIE DEFEZ, BEL** aureliedefez.eu	052	**GRAPHEINE.COM, FRA** @grapheine_branding grapheine.com	E p. 174
NADINE BELA, DEU @belabiene	004	**LENA ZOE DERNAI, DEU** @_nspken_	003	**TIM GRÜTZNER, DEU** @timgruetzner timgruetzner.com	009
MAXIME A. METZELER / **BELLAVENDER, CHE** @maxblvndr bellavender.com	013	**LISELOTTE DIER, DEU** @lisolette_d	082	**LUKAS HAIDER, AUT** @lkshdr lukashaider.com	094
KYLIÈN BERGH, NLD kylienbergh.nl	E p. 193	**DISPLAAY, CZE** @xyz_displaay displaay.net	121	**HANSEL GROTESQUE** **STUDIO, ITA** @hanselgrotesquestudio hansel-grotesque.it	078
FLORIAN BEYELER, CHE @florianbeyeler florianbeyeler.ch	045	**MILAN DOCTOR, DEU** @iamdoctormilan	058	**HARDAL STUDIO, TUR** @_hardal hardalstudio.com	133
CHEN LUO / **BODY&FORMA,** **USA** @bodyandforma chenluodesign.net	035	**PAULA DONATH, DEU** @pauladnth pauladonath.de	028	**PADDY HARTLEY, GBR** @paddyhartleyartist paddyhartley.com	051
		MAIKE C. DORN, DEU @maikecdorn	007	**JIMMY HENDERSON, USA** @jimmytheink jimmyhendersonstudio.com	E 190
		JELENA DROBAC, SRB @d.ideashop d-ideashop.com	E p. 178	**ALENA HERMES, DEU** @godsdeliverygirl	116

FRANÇOISE HOFFMANN, FRA francoisehoffmann.fr	030 031	**EIKE KÖNIG, DEU** 081 @eikekoenig eikekonig.com
LUCA HOLZINGER, FRA 065 @lucaholzinger lucaholzinger.com		**JUDITH KÖNIGSTEIN, DEU** 101 @judith.koenigstein
ANNA HORVÁTH, HUN 008 @horvathann		**LISA KONNO, NLD** 059 @lisakonno lisakonno.com
DAHYUN HWANG, DEU 098 @da_hyonni dahyunhwang.com		**ANNE KRAFT, DEU** 097
JUAN VALENTIN-GAMAZO / JUAN VG, ESP 067 @juanvgdesigner juanvgdesigner.com		**SOFIA KRIKLII, KAZ** 022 @sofya.frash
		MARKUS LANGE, DEU 134 @markus_lange markuslange.co
KENDALL ROSS / I'D KNIT THAT, USA 093 @id.knit.that idknitthatco.com		**LATINOTYPE, CHL** 122 @latinotype latinotype.com
NESSIM HIGSON / IAAH, NLD 062 @nessimhigson 063 iaah.work		**PABLO LEHMANN, ARG** 073 @pablo_lehmann pablolehmann.com.ar
ERMAN YILMAZ / INFORMAL PROJECT 099 @informalproject.co informalproject.co		**LESLEY DILL / LESLEY DILL STUDIO, USA** 069 @lesleydill1 071, 072 lesleydill.net
MARIE JANSEN, DEU 028 @localgingerbitch		**ANNIKA LOTTER, DEU** 032 @annika_lotter annikalotter.com
CHARLOTTE JESCHINA, DEU 119 @c_js_pro_jects		**ANTON ABO / M0D44, UKR** 029 @anton_abo m0d44.com
KD26 A, NLD 076 @kd26_label kd-26.com		**MARC ARMAND / MARC ARMAND WORKS / FEELINGS, FRA** 054 @marc_is_tsq marcarmand-works.com
VOLODYMYR KHOMENKO, UKR 096 @adultero_vagabond behance.net/khkhomenko		**MAX MÄDER, DEU** 010 @maedermax
SAN KIM, KOR 061 @sankim_official		**RICCARDO MATLAKAS, GBR** 068 @riccardo_matlakas matlakas.co.uk
VIKTORIA KLOTZ, DEU 111 @fbg_students design.h-da.de		**JAKOB MAYER, DEU** 097
STELLA KLUMP, DEU 036 @stella.klump		**JOHANNA MEHNER, DEU** 113 @_HANNARA_
KNIFE KNIFE, GBR 066 @0411knife		**KUBA SOWIŃSKI / MOST, POL** 033 @themostpl 048 themost.pl
ILYA KOERS, BEL 024 @ilyakoers ilyakoers.myportfolio.com		kubasowinski.myportfolio.com/work

MUK MONSALVE, LUCHEE SOTO / MUSA DEL ASFALTO, ARG	027
@musadelasfalto musadelasfalto.com.ar	
KEVIN NOWAK, PARTERRE, AUT	060
@kevinxnowak @parterre.cc parterre.cc	
ORTNER ETC., AUT	107, 108
@ortneretc ortneretc.com	111
OTOG STUDIO, GBR	053
@otogstudio otogstudio.com	
JULIUS PFEUFFER, DEU	046
@julius.pfeuffer wtfiq.net	
ANNA PIERCY, GBR	074
NICOLAS PORTNOÏ, FRA	047
@nicolas_portnoi nicolasportnoi.fr	
ISMAHANE POUSSIN, FRA	005
@psmahane	
JEAN-BAPTISTE LEVÉE / PRODUCTION TYPE, FRA	077, 123 124, 127
productiontype.com	I, p. 214
MARK CANESO / PS TYPE, USA	089, 091
@markcaneso pstypelab.com	
PUBLIC POSSESSION, DEU	083
@public_possession publicpossession.com	
MARY Y. YANG / RADICAL CHARACTERS, USA	035
@radicalcharacters radicalcharacters.org	
NATALIA RATAJCZAK, POL	102
@duet_zezowaty nratajczak.pl	
RAYMUNDO T. REYNOSO, USA	040
@eyeone_sh eyeonestudio.com	
PHILIP RUDZINSKI, DEU	039
@rudjeanski	
LUIS RUTZ, DEU	118
@luis_rutz luisrutz.de	

KARMEN SAMSON, NLD — E
karmensamson.com — p. 193

SCHICK TOIKKA — 125, 126
FLORIAN SCHICK,
LAURI TOIKKA, DEU / FIN
@schicktoikka
schick-toikka.com

ROBERTO SCHNEEBERGER, — 104
STUDIO 5115 SNC, CHE
@roby_swiss
5115.studio

JULIA SCHRÖDER, DEU — 034
@juliadesines
design.h-da.de

JELENA SCHÜLLER, DEU — 014
@jxleua

LUIS SCHULTE KELLINGHAUS, — 097
DEU
@lu.sk

CHRISTINA DONOGHUE / — E
SHOWSTUDIO, GBR — p. 162
showstudio.com/contributors/
christina-donoghue

SERGEY SKIP, DEU — 080
@sergeyskip.visuals
sergeyskip.com

NADINE SLEIMAN, DEU — 049
@nadineslmn
nadinesleiman.com

ROWENA STAFFORD, IRL — 106

STUDIO FABIO BIESEL, — 120
DEU
@studiofabiobiesel
studiofabiobiesel.com

GOLNAR KAT-RAHMANI / — 110
STUDIO GOLNAR — I, p. 202
KATRAHMANI, DEU
@golnarkat
katrahmani.com

LUCAS HESSE / — 038
STUDIO LUCAS HESSE, DEU
@_hesselucas
lucas-hesse.de

OMID NEMALHABIB / — 018
STUDIO MELLI, NLD
@studiomelli
studio-melli.com

MICHAEL SATTER / STUDIO — 015
MICHAEL SATTER, DEU
@studiomichaelsatter
michaelsatter.de

STUDIO NIKOLAI DOBREFF, — 012
DEU
@nikolaidobreff
nikolaidobreff.de

STUDIO TEMP, ITA — 037
@studiotemp
temp.studio

SYLVAIN, FRA — 121
@ sylvainlabs
sylvain.co

HAILEE TALBOT, USA — 070
haileetalbot.com

CIHAN TAMTI, DEU — 112
@cihantamti
cihan-tamti.de

TATJANA HAUPT / — 001
TATI THINGS,
DEU
@tati_things_
tati-things.com

TEST PRINT, CHE — 042
@testprint.z

RÜDIGER SCHLÖMER, — 044
TYPEKNITTING, CHE
@typeknitting
typeknitting.net

XIXI TONG, GBR — 066
@xi.scorpii.official

GIANPAOLO TUCCI, DEU — 114
@aesthetics_imperfections
gianpaolotucci.com

MARTIN FUSSENEGGER, — I
JOCHEN SMUDA / — p. 210
UCON ACROBATICS,
DEU
@ucon_acrobatics
ucon-acrobatics.com

VERA VAN DE SEYP, — 056
NED / USA
@veravandeseyp
veravandeseyp.com

STÉPHANIE VILAYPHIOU / — 006
VVVVV, BEL
@vvvvvilay
gitlab.com/svilayphiou

LOÏC VOLKART, CHE — 105
@loicvolkart
black-box-is-orange.com

VINCENT WAGNER, AUT — 100
@computer_vincent
vincent.computer

ANN MARIE WAINSCOTT, — E
USA — p. 169
annmariewainscott.com

MARIE WALSER, DEU — 050
@hi.webad
we-bad.com

BLANCA WILL, DEU — 055
@blanca.will.design

SAMUEL RHODES / — 043
WEEKEND ROMANCE, JPN
@week.end.romance
samuelrhodes.com

IAN LYNAM / WORDSHAPE, — 043
JPN — E
@ianlynam — p. 185
ianlynam.com

YOTAFONTS — 128
@YOTAFONTS
yotafonts.com

SLANTED MAGAZINE
TYPOGRAPHY & DESIGN CULTURE
AUTUMN / WINTER 2024 / 25
44 TYPE FASHION

PUBLISHER

Slanted Publishers UG
(haftungsbeschränkt)
Nördliche Uferstraße 4–6
76189 Karlsruhe
Germany
T +49 (0) 721 85 14 82 68
magazine@slanted.de
slanted.de

TEAM

Editor in Chief (V.i.S.d.P.)
 Lars Harmsen
Co-Editor
 Greta Landmann
Managing Editor
 Julia Kahl
Creative Direction
 Lars Harmsen
Graphic Design
 Greta Landmann, Juliane Lipp
Final Design
 Julia Kahl, Juliane Lipp
Cover Image: W:A.R. by Walter van Beirendonck,
photographed by Ronald Stoops

SLANTED WEBLOG

Editor in Chief (V.i.S.d.P.)
 Julia Kahl
Editors
 slanted.de/editors

VIDEO

Video Interviews
slanted.de/videos

ISBN: 978-3-948440-76-3
ISSN 1867-6510
Frequency 2 × p. a.
(Spring / Summer, Autumn / Winter)

Copyright
© Slanted Publishers, 2024
Nördliche Uferstraße 4–6, 76189 Karlsruhe
Germany
All rights reserved.

PRODUCTION

Printing
 Stober Medien GmbH
 Eggenstein / Germany
 stober-medien.de

Bookbinder
 Buchbinderei Spinner
 Ottersweier / Germany
 josef-spinner.de

Cardboard Cover
 WestRock Crescendo® C1S 340 g / sm
Paper Inside
 arto®gloss 150 g / sm
 Iona®offset 110 g / sm
Distributed by
 Inapa Deutschland
 Hamburg / Germany
 inapa.de

Spot Colors
 HKS Warenzeichenverband e. V.
 Stuttgart / Germany
 hks-farben.de
 HKS 13, HKS 43

Fonts

OPS Noise Abroad, 2020
Design: Our Polite Society & Jan Egbers
Label: Our Polite Society Type /
ourpolitesocietytype.net

Proxima Soft, 2017
Design: Mark Simonson
Label: Mark Simonson Studio / marksimonson.com

RYM, 2022
Design: Fabiola Mejía
Label: Supercontinente / supercontinente.com

Suisse Int'l, 2011
Design: Swiss Typefaces Design Team
Label: Swiss Typefaces / swisstypefaces.com

DISCLAIMER

The publisher assumes no responsibility for the accuracy of all information. Publisher and editor assume that material that was made available for publishing, is free of third party rights. Reproduction and storage require the permission of the publisher. Photos and texts are welcome, but there is no liability. Signed contributions do not necessarily represent the opinion of the publisher or the editor.

The German National Library lists this publication in the German National Bibliography; detailed bibliographic data is available on the Internet at dnb.de

SUBSCRIPTIONS

Subscribe to Slanted Magazine and support what we do. Magazines via subscriptions are at a reduced rate and get shipped directly at release, for free within Germany.
slanted.de/subscription

2-Issues-Subscription
€ 40.– + shipping
4-Issues-Subscription
€ 80.– + shipping
Student Subscription
2 issues for € 37.– + shipping
Gift Subscription
2 issues wrapped as present for € 42.– + shipping
2-Issues-Subscritpion + related Special Editions
2 issues + 2 special editions for € 60.– + shipping
4-Issues-Subscritpion + related Special Editions
4 issues + 4 special editions + free issue
for € 120.– + shipping

SALES AND DISTRIBUTION

Slanted Magazine can be purchased online, in selected bookstores, concept stores, and galleries worldwide. If you own a shop and would like to stock Slanted Magazine or other publications from us, please get in touch:

Contact / Distribution DE
Julia Klose, T +49 (0) 721 85148268
julia.klose@slanted.de
Distribution UK
Public Knowledge Books /
publicknowledgebooks.com
Distribution US
Small Changes / smallchanges.com
Distribution EU & WORLD
Idea Books / ideabooks.nl
Slanted Shop
slanted.de/shop
Retail & Distribution
slanted.de/distribution

ADVERTISING

We offer a wide range of advertising possibilities online and in print. For advertising inquiries please get in touch with:
Julia Kahl (advertising management / sales)
+49 (0) 721 851 482 68, julia.kahl@slanted.de
slanted.de/publisher/advertising

AWARDS (SELECTION)

ADC of Europe
ADC Germany
Annual Multimedia
Berliner Type
DDC
Designpreis der BRD
European Design Awards
Faces of Design Awards
iF communication design award
German Design Award
Laus Awards
Lead Awards (Weblog des Jahres & Visual Leader)
red dot communication design awards
Type Directors Club NY
Tokyo Type Directors Club
Werkbund Label

ACKNOWLEDGEMENT

We would like to thank everyone who followed our call for submissions online in spring 2024 and submitted hundreds of graphics, artworks, fashion pieces, and texts. It was not easy to make a selection. Unfortunately, due to the limited scope, we could not depict every work. We hope that for those who did not make it into the magazine, there will be another opportunity in the future.

A huge thank you to Greta Landmann for writing countless emails and assisting with editing and design. It was a pleasure working with you!

With this issue, we're excited to offer a limited edition of crossbody bags with a statement, made from 95 % recycled materials by the Berlin-based label Ucon Acrobatics (see interview on p. 210). These exclusive bags are only available in a bundle with this issue in our online shop at slanted.de/product/limited-special-edition-type-fashion — a big thank you to Martin Fussenegger & Jochen Smuda. Join the SLW FSHN CLB!

Thanks to Golnar Kat-Rahmani, Jochen Smuda and Martin Fussenegger, Mirko Borsche, and Jean-Baptiste Levée for conducting an interview with us despite the lack of time and vacation.

Many thanks to Florian Brugger for connecting us with Valentino from Public Possession.

Special thanks to Walter van Beirendonck. We spent ages working on a cover and then we got these great photos. You made our day!

This issue has been printed on different, great papers—thank you, Michaela Deckelmann (Inapa Deutschland) for your uncomplicated, kind support!

Thanks to our printing partner Stober Medien near Karlsruhe for the perfect printing of this magazine. Thank you, Marcus Grunvinck and the whole team!

A special thanks to our supporters and fans out there. You help a lot, sharing our work to the world, making Slanted a wonderful community of design interested people. We love you!

Last but not least: Thanks to everyone who is against fast fashion, dresses consciously and supports sustainable labels.

134—MARKUS LANGE FOR SLANTED PUBLISHERS
DEU
BOOK READER

Show your love for books with this exclusive piece from our new SLNTD CLB collection. The bold "Book Reader" design proudly displays your passion for books. Join the club—J*N TH CLB! Available exclusively in the Slanted Shop slanted.de/product/slntd-clb-book-reader